BABYLON · MEMPHIS · PERSEPOLIS

BABYLON

∽

MEMPHIS

∽

PERSEPOLIS

*Eastern Contexts of
Greek Culture*

WALTER BURKERT

HARVARD UNIVERSITY PRESS
*Cambridge, Massachusetts
London, England*

First Harvard University Press paperback edition, 2007

Library of Congress Cataloging-in-Publication Data

Burkert, Walter, 1931–

Babylon, Memphis, Persepolis : eastern contexts of Greek culture / Walter Burkert.

p.   cm.

Includes bibliographical references and index.

ISBN-13 978-0-674-01489-3 (cloth: alk. paper)

ISBN-10 0-674-01489-8 (cloth: alk. paper)

ISBN-13 978-0-674-02399-4 (pbk.)

ISBN-10 0-674-02399-4 (pbk.)

1. Greek literature—Oriental influences.   2. Greece—Civilization—Oriental influences.
3. Homer—Knowledge—Middle East.   4. Middle East—In literature.
5. Magi.   I. Title.

PA 3070.B75 2004

880'.9001—dc22   2004047412

Preface

In April 1996, I presented four lectures on early Oriental-Greek interactions at the Università Ca Foscari of Venice. Professors Claudia Antonetti and Lucio Milano took the initiative to transform these *Lezioni Veneziane* into a small book, which was published with the title *Da Omero ai Magli* by Marsilio Editori in 1999. Growing interest led to a French, a Spanish, and a German edition: *La tradition orientale dans la culture grecque,* Paris: Macula 2001; *De Homero a los Magos,* Barcelona: El Acantilado 2002; *Die Griechen und der Orient,* Munich: Beck 2003.

As against the original lectures, the text of the book has been reworked and expanded. I added a general introduction and a chapter on writing, and brought in new material and insights, especially in Chapter 4. At present, Eastern cultures, which were a marginal curiosity for classicists until recently, have become a field of intensive international research and debate; the list of publications keeps expanding. My intention in this book has been to preserve the advantage of lectures to concentrate on the presentation of ideas and interpretations; the endnotes can only touch the surface of a vast scholarship.

My thanks go to Margaretta Fulton, Anita Safran, and to Harvard University Press in general, for their initiative, stimulus, and all their help in the English edition.

Contents

BABYLON · MEMPHIS · PERSEPOLIS

Introduction

The Cyclopes, Homer observes, are savages just because of their isolation: "For the Cyclopes do not have ships . . . as elsewhere men travel to each other by ships across the sea."[1] Hence they live in a kind of natural paradise, without agriculture, viticulture, city, or state, like lawless ogres. Civilization, by contrast, develops through contact with foreigners and distant partners, mainly by way of travel and commerce. Interaction gives people the chance "to see the cities of many humans, and to learn about their minds,"[2] as Homer says in praise of Odysseus right at the start of the *Odyssey*. Culture, including Greek culture, requires intercultural contact.

European tradition, especially the scholarly tradition, used to see the Greeks in a different perspective, as unique and isolated, classical. "Classical" presupposes and confirms recognized standards or norms—but these are disappearing from our multicultural world and will not be recovered easily. A term such as Classical Greece may still be usable, nay convenient, as it refers to a civilization that was superior in the sense that it became a model imitated throughout the Mediterranean and beyond, in the East and in the Latin West, and was rediscovered as a model several times afterwards in periods of renaissance. For good reason Europe bears a Greek name. And the Greek heritage has been hardly less important for Islam.

"Classical," however, does not connote isolation. Other periods may have had an interest in insisting on distinctions. The Renaissance, for example, made the admiration of classical antiquity a program of self-definition, adding to it the historical perspective of Gothic decline and resurgence of humane civilization. The Enlightenment went further, with the concept of intellectual progress starting from classical antiquity. In consequence, Classical Greece was made to appear as an "origin," naturally sprouting, as it were, from the seeds of unique talents.

New interest in historical research in the nineteenth century established the isolation of classical Greece all the more.[3] The Napoleonic wars had ended with a surge of nationalism, especially in Germany. Subsequently it was taken for granted that culture had to be national culture. Just at that time Indoeuropean linguistics were discovered and elaborated, bringing Greeks, Romans, and Germanic tribes together and building up a barrier between them and the Semites, the Hebrews of the Old Testament.[4] Homer, who had been declared an "original genius" in the eighteenth century,[5] now became the genius of Hellenic origins; for Germany, this meant an alliance of German, Greek, and Protestant, which was largely to dominate the school system, the "gymnasium" of the nineteenth century.

In consequence, Hellenic scholarship largely failed to recognize the sensational progress made in the nineteenth century in the study of antiquity upon the rediscovery of the ancient Near East. The decipherment of hieroglyphs and cuneiform added about two millennia to our historical record; it opened up the earliest high cultures in their original languages. Parallel to the discovery of forgotten literature great excavations were made in Egypt and in Mesopotamia (1842–1855), then in Greece. The results were rich and startling. Yet the special disciplines that were developing in this way, Near Eastern, Egyptian, Old Testament, and Classical Greek studies, naturally tended to differentiate and become fields of specialized competence. A comprehensive view like that of Eduard Meyer was an exception.[6]

New impulses came from new discoveries in the twentieth century. Beginning in 1915, the Hittite language and civilization in Central Anatolia became accessible, along with the huge archive of Boghazköy-Hattusa; in Syria, Ugarit, with Ugaritic archives, was excavated and the language deciphered by Semitists about 1930.[7] Both discoveries brought the East into direct touch with the ancient Greeks, both in Asia Minor and at the Mediterranean coast. As Hittite proved to be a member of the Indoeuopean language family, the Greek/Semite division turned out to be invalid in this case. Some Eastern parallels to Greek mythology made a special impact: in 1930 Walter Porzig wrote on "Illuyankas and Typhon," comparing a dragon figure of Hittite mythology with the Greek monster Typhon, and in 1935 Forrer published the first research results on Kumarbi, a deity who evidently corresponds to Kronos in Hesiod's *Theogony.*[8] Yet among classical philologists only Franz Dornseiff, playing the outsider, realized the new dimensions of the ancient world and proposed giving up the dogma of "provincial seclusion" of civilizations in the early Iron Age.[9] This idea found more general resonance only after the end of World War II. In 1946, the Hittite "Kingdom in Heaven" was published,[10] and nobody could deny that this text was quite close to Hesiod's *Theogony*—and, of course, considerably older. Then, in 1952–53, the decipherment of Linear B presented Greek from Bronze Age Greece and Crete.[11] This engendered considerable enthusiasm for the Bronze Age even among classicists, as seen in the publications of T. B. L. Webster and Denys Page; Cyrus Gordon coined the catchword of a "Bronze age *koine*" (that is, common understanding within a common civilization).[12] Alfred Heubeck, though, insisted on the chronological distance and the differences between Mycenae and Homer, and drew attention to post-Bronze Age developments and contacts.[13]

More recently, intercultural perspectives are on the winning side, while the traditional picture of Greek origins appears more and more distant and pale. The background for this change may be the critical situation of European culture as a whole in the developing world society. Europeans are a dwindling minority, as the United States marks its distance from European origins and elaborates a future of its own. Aggressive criticism has derided the prerogatives of "dead white men," of which the ancient Greeks might well be the oldest, and hence more dead than the others. Martin Bernal achieved enormous success with his book *Black Athena: The Afroasianic Roots of Classical Civilization*,[14] in which he accuses traditional European scholarship, and German scholarship most of all, of having neglected or obscured the cultural achievements of the south and the east, especially of Bronze Age Egypt. Vigorous debates have ensued; yet while many details of Bernal and his followers' statements are open to argument, polemics are not worthwhile. One ought to look for further evidence and new perspectives, and to work out more equitable judgments.[15]

No doubt our traditional use of the term "Eastern" or "Oriental" presupposes a "Western" perspective, as if the countries and civilizations that lie more or less east or southeast of Europe— Asia Minor, Iraq, Iran, Syria, Palestine, and Egypt—had ever been a unity and not a complex plurality of regions and cultures. Still, in general terms (and excluding the Far East), we can agree that it was there that the first high cultures developed and spread their achievements to neighboring regions. The background and context of the so-called Greek miracle, if there ever was one, is to be found there. So in the chapters that follow the cultural environment of early Greek civilization will be approached from the side of its eastern neighbors.

This does not mean that we can explain much of cultural development in a causal way. Causal explanations of complex cultural phenomena will always remain tentative and one-sided. Yet a more dimensional view will yield more adequate descriptions. Hence the dynamics of cultural interaction will be in focus here. It is true that the mere statement of influence is unsatisfactory. One has to seek out the kinds of response to cultural influence, the modifications that occurred, including possible progress by misunderstanding. We shall meet both with positive input, such as the transfer of technology, skills, and ideas in a large sense, and also with negative input, such as invasion, oppression, and exploitation. The main question will be how and how much were the existing social and economic systems affected by such events, whether they were brought to further development or else inhibited and destroyed in the process. The facts of history are unforeseeable, but they cannot be overlooked in retrospect.

Greece is insufficiently defined by geography.[16] Already in the Bronze Age Greeks had moved beyond the Balkan Peninsula on to the Aegean islands, Crete and Cyprus, along the coast of Asia Minor, and even south Italy and Sicily. There were contacts and interactions on all sides. But whereas the West passively elicited the search for raw materials, especially metals, and offered space for agriculture, the Eastern high cultures that had been developing in Egypt and in Mesopotamia, with Syria-Palestine between them and Anatolia right to the side, took the lead in interaction. These civilizations were distinguished by a high state of organization, including the use of writing and a power system centered on kings and temples. They had arisen in the third millennium; they had a complicated history with ups and downs, flourishing and demise, during the second millennium (we usually speak of the Middle and the Late Bronze Age); they still dominated the beginnings of the Iron Age.

The Bronze Age system swept to Europe to become the first

European high culture, namely the Minoan, which flourished in Crete in the first half of the second millennium. It centered on palaces such as Knossos, Phaistos, Mallia, and Kydonia (Chania) for administration and economic activities, with a writing system, Linear A, that remains undeciphered. This culture reached mainland Greece by about 1600 B.C., with palaces at Mycenae, Pylos, and Thebes; their script, Linear B, deciphered in 1952, was Mycenaean Greek.[17]

Most Bronze Age civilizations around the Aegean collapsed about 1200 B.C. in a strange catastrophe that struck Greece, Crete, Hittite Anatolia, Syria, and Palestine. Palaces, large stone architecture, and even metalwork practically disappeared for some centuries; several writing systems fell out of use and were forgotten. Less affected were Egypt and Mesopotamia; catastrophes and continuities alike happened at Cyprus. The details and reasons for this multiple catastrophe are obscured by the breakdown of literacy; guesswork and hypotheses are left—invasions or economic failure, social upheaval, plague or drought?[18]

A new world gradually emerged around the eastern Mediterranean, with Philistines in Palestine, flourishing coastal cities such as Tyre and Sidon in Phoenicia, small dynasties of Aramaeans and Luwians that ruled from northern Syria to Anatolia, a major kingdom of Phrygians farther northwest, another powerful kingdom, Urartu, toward the east in what is now Armenia. At that time three dominating factors wrought change, progress, and crisis: the development of maritime trade, which turned toward the western Mediterranean in search of metals, was carried on with growing success by the Phoenicians and later by the Greeks; the onset of military power of the Assyrians; and the expansion of an easy writing system, the alphabet, which took literacy out of the hands of royal or temple bureaucrats and made it available to the enterprising individual. The interplay of these factors caused the center of civilization to shift westward from the Near East to the Mediterranean. And the nearest Westerners were the Greeks. They immediately benefited—they got their chance, and their "miracle."[19]

Some words about Assyria first. It was an old tradition in Mesopotamia that the king should be called Lord of the Whole, Lord of the Four Quarters of the World. But the kings of Assur administered these titles in a new key. Organizing superior military power, they began to conquer and to plunder their neighbors, the adjacent tribes, kingdoms, or cities, in a systematic way year after year; they took booty and imposed devastating tribute and thus could maintain their superior army. Beginning in the ninth century they expanded westward, toward Syria: Assurnasirpal reached the Mediterranean. The climax came in the eighth and seventh centuries: Damascus was conquered about 800, Israel in 722, Cyprus about 700, where king Sargon left his stele with a cuneiform inscription;[20] there was a naval battle between Ionians and Assyrians near Tarsus in Cilicia about 700;[21] Sidon was destroyed in 672; Egypt came under Assyrian domination between 671 and 655. Jerusalem was saved through diplomacy for once. The main adversary of Assyria in eastern Anatolia, Urartu, collapsed under a northern invasion by Cimmerians about 700; so did Phrygia.[22] At that time Gyges, well known to the Greeks, became king of Lydia. He could make use of the growing gold production in that region[23] and was certainly remembered by the Greeks for his gold.[24] The Greek cities in Asia Minor, one after the other, succumbed to his power. He sought recognition from the East and made an alliance with Assurbanipal, king of Assyria, who in turn considered him his vassal.[25] Whatever the precise nature of their relation, a direct road from Asia Minor to Mesopotamian Nineveh had been explored by then and was established for current use; it was subsequently called the King's Road.

Invasions and conquests are not a popular topic in modern historiography. Still, one cannot overlook their disastrous consequences for the cultural development of peoples. Luwians, Aramaeans, Phoenicians, and Israelites were really afflicted for several generations. The Greeks, however, were fortunate to be touched but not crushed by the onslaught. Being the most eastern of the Westerners, they were mainly affected in a positive way.

Material riches come from trade rather than from military incursions. The Phoenicians, mainly from Sidon and Tyre, were the first to develop long-distance trade in the Mediterranean[26] with luxury items such as purple dye and perfumes, but also with metals; their trade reached the Greek islands[27] and also the cities on the continent. Skilled craftsmen came too, quite a few probably as refugees from the Assyrian devastations, and they brought with them more solid refinements of Eastern civilization, such as bronze work and large-scale architecture, ivory carving, and production of terracottas from molds. Eventually the Greeks succeeded in developing long-distance trade themselves, side by side with the Phoenicians and in competition with them, from Syria via Crete to Sicily and Etruria, with colonies in southern Italy and in Sicily. Crete and Rhodes had been stopovers and centers of trade in the earlier period, in the eighth century. Euboea held a dominant place in this trade, to be overtaken by Corinth for Western connections, especially when Cercyra had become Greek. Ionia, on the eastern side, profited from land trade along the King's Road, following the initiative of Gyges.[28] In fact the kingdom of Lydia must have served as a connecting link between Assyria and Greeks for nearly a century.[29] Beginning in the seventh century Ionians developed ties to Egypt,[30] but also went north to establish a hold in Thrace and along the Black Sea through their colonies. The Greek activities meant competition and collaboration with the Phoenicians, who, however, suffered at home ever more severely from Assyrian incursions; this caused the Phoenician center to shift from Tyre to Carthage.

Assyrian power reached its climax with the conquest of Egypt

(671–655); the reign of Assurbanipal (668–631) brought a period of peace and stability and a general rise of welfare. Assurbanipal was the only Assyrian king who learned to write and read; he established the library at Nineveh which later proved to be a treasure trove for Assyriology. One new form of luxury behavior that began to spread at his time from Assyria via Lydia to Ionia and to the Greeks in general was the use of *klinai,* couches for reclining at the symposium. The key piece of evidence is a relief from Nineveh, termed "Assurbanipal's garden party"; it became a type of iconography directly copied by the Greeks.[31]

Not long after Assurbanipal's death, however, the power of Assyria was annihilated by the combined attack of Babylonians and Iranian Medes. Nineveh was conquered and totally destroyed in 612 B.C.; 200 years later Xenophon, passing the ruins at the site, heard some fantastic tales, but nothing approaching history, not even the name of the place.[32]

Greeks must have come to know about these dramatic events as onlookers, as it were, at the fringe. The verse of Phocylides warning against "silly Ninos" may be of dubious authenticity.[33] But the "country Iaunaia" (Ionia) and even some individuals of that country show up in Assyrian documents even before the fall of Nineveh.[34] Greek merchants seem to have settled in Syria by the ninth century,[35] and it is very likely that Greek mercenaries joined the Assyrian armies.[36] About 738 a cuneiform letter from Syria mentions invaders from "the country Iaunaia," that is, Ionians who had plundered the Syrian coast.[37] It must have been about that time that Greeks came into possession of some beautiful pieces of bronze horse harness, which had belonged to Hazael, king of Damascus about 800, as an Aramaic inscription tells us. Were they gifts given by high-ranking aristocrats, or just mercenaries' booty? The Greeks dedicated them to Hera of Samos and to Apollo of Eretria.[38] At that time Ionians fought a naval battle with Assyrians,[39] while Assyrians invaded Cyprus and made

Greek "kings" pay tribute to the Great King.[40] The rich and startling finds from royal tombs at Salamis on Cyprus, which suggested Homeric style to the excavators, come from the period of
Assyrian sovereignty.[41] Yet Greek settlements remained immune,
as far as we can see, from devastating destruction which befell
Luwians and Aramaeans, Phoenicians, Egypt, and also Israel and
Jerusalem.

The short apogee of Babylonia under king Nebukadnezar
(604–562) after the fall of Nineveh brought the destruction of Jerusalem in 586, but just marginally affected the Greeks. The
brother of the poet Alcaeus, Antimenidas, served as a mercenary
at Babylon at the time.[42] This brings the name of the far-away
metropolis into a Greek text for the first time. Closer to home
and more important was that Egypt, which had regained its inde-
pendence with king Psammetichus, rose to power in the eastern
Mediterranean and established close contacts with Greeks. Greek
mercenaries had been instrumental in Psammetichus' insurrection and found further fields of activities.[43] Pedon, a Greek from
Priene, had earned special merit with king Psammetichus and received "a golden bracelet and a city" for his "manliness"; he set up
a basalt monument of typical Egyptian style to celebrate his glory.
The inscription is in Greek but echoes Egyptian practice and values.[44] More general profit came from trade connections: Greek
cities in and around the Aegean and Asia Minor were allowed to
establish permanent settlements in Egyptian Naukratis. Herodotus enumerates 11 cities that had dependencies there, including
Samos and Chios;[45] the site was established before Amasis, as excavations proved. At that time Cyprus too began to assume an
Egyptian orientation. Probably the most important import that
was available thereafter and which became an unalienable constituent of Greek civilization was papyrus, the convenient writing
material for documents, letters, and book scrolls. The heavy and
expensive leather scrolls that had been in use since the advent of

writing were definitely supplanted by papyrus during or after the seventh century.

The special luck at the fringes of the imperial East, which had made the Assyrian epoch a period of progress and efflorescence for the Greeks, was repeated, in a striking and unforeseeable way, when the next and much better organized empire, the Achaemenid empire, made its appearance. It stopped its expansion at the Greek world, right at the borderline that has since been called the frontier between Asia and Europe. This moment of history, the Persian Wars (500–479), has become so famous that we tend to forget how paradoxical and unforeseeable it must have been. We do not even know how things looked from the East; Persian sources are lost, and the Hebrews, whose literature survived, were uninterested in what happened to the Jawan, as they called the Greeks. They remained grateful to king Cyrus, who had allowed them to refound Judaea as a theocratic vassal state in Palestine. As for the Greeks, roughly one third of them, those in Anatolia, came under Persian domination and lost their cultural importance for centuries; but the rest unexpectedly succeeded in retaining liberty and hence developed a new self-consciousness in opposition to the East. This is proclaimed in the tragedy entitled *Persians,* staged by Aeschylus at Athens in 472: Greeks against *barbaroi,* Europe against Asia, freedom against slavery, fighters against effeminates, order of the gods against the insolence of tyranny. This was the advent of what has since been called classical civilization.[46] In consequence, Athens became the cultural capital of Greece, and the Attic dialect acquired the status of the leading language of Greek literature. When, 300 years later, the Western empire, the Romans, came to conquer the whole of Greece, the Greeks had long had their apogee and had immortalized it through splendid artwork and literature that was to persist.

*   *   *

"Whatever the Greeks take over from the barbarians, they make better." This statement from the Platonic *Epinomis* (987d) has been quoted perhaps too often, already before the Orient became known to any depth, and all the more since then. We have perhaps become more hesitant to judge civilizations by criteria of better or worse. But it is the relation of model and imitation that justifies the metaphor of higher versus lower culture and objectively shows cultural influence flowing from one source to another. And yet in the process of acculturation something new may arise; and although Greeks had been on the receiving side for a long time, there is no doubt that the result is Greek. It is Greek art and architecture that have become classical, and Greek literature that has become world literature.

Take a look at the situation at about 500 B.C. By then Etruscans would use Greek myths for the pictures on their vases and metal work, adding inscriptions with the Greek names; Romans accepted Greek gods, the Dioscures, which they named Castores, for worship at the Forum and built a temple for them, and they also took over the cult of Apollo, without changing his name. Meanwhile, in the East, king Darius summoned Greek sculptors to decorate Persepolis, his new capital, built for the New Year ceremony. Red-figure ceramics from Attica circulated not only around the Mediterranean but as far as central Germany. Greek style had become a model for the whole of the Mediterranean world, both in artistic craftsmanship and in mythological poetry; it even had its effects in the East. In a way it was already dominating world civilization, and this without the props of military or political power.

Things had been different 200 years earlier. At that time the Orient—Anatolia, Mesopotamia, Syria—clearly was superior, and currents of influence moved from East to West. For Greece this meant progress. Technical skills came from the East, bronze work notably and large-scale architecture, which had practically become extinct in Greece after the breakdown of the Mycenaean system, just as literacy had been forgotten. Greek craftsmanship was on the move, as can be seen in protogeometric ceramics, yet the geometric forms were enriched by the orientalizing style of the eighth and seventh centuries. Oriental models were felt to be attractive, nay superior, whether Phoenician, Syrian/Urartaean/Assyrian, or Egyptian. At a certain stage it is difficult to distinguish Urartaean/Syrian bronze tripods from Greek ones, as both were brought into Greek sanctuaries, which were growing richer. But then Greek craftsmen definitely outgrew their Eastern masters; and Urartu fell victim to the Cimmerian invasions and disappeared.

A new and special impact on large stonework came from Egypt toward the end of the seventh century. Characteristic is the figure of the standing young male, the *kouros* type: it comes in the canonic forms of Lower Egypt. One notable difference is that Greek *kouroi* are provocatively naked; and nudity was to become one of the strongest influences in the legacy of Greek art. No doubt it was the development of Greek sports which is reflected in this convention. Earlier, a nude goddess had arrived from Syria, represented in relief plates and seals, both in clay and in metal, eagerly copied by Greeks. But it was only in Crete that a few attempts were made to transform this model into large temple sculptures, such as those at Prinias and Gortyn. The nude female disappeared again from Greek art for centuries, whereas the nude male in his Egyptian posture was to dominate.[47] Greek civilization had made its distinct selection.

Even more important was the Greek temple, which developed toward its definite forms after the end of the seventh century.[48] It has a complicated pedigree. Neither Minoans nor Mycenaeans built temples as such, though they had various forms of sanctuaries; nor did the sub-Minoan sanctuaries of Crete, with their remarkable clay statues, find successors.[49] The idea of the "great house" of the gods—Sumerian E-Gal—clearly is at home with the old high cultures of the East, with various conventional forms of temples in Syria and Palestine. This idea took on the Mycenaean style at Cyprus by the twelfth century, with impressive bronze figurines which we used to believe were cult statues.[50] In Greece and on the islands, worship of the gods lacked temples for a long time; there is no undisputed evidence for such buildings before the ninth century. Then builders began to experiment with various forms at Crete and Aetolia, Samos and Ephesus. The Greek name is *naos, neos,* apparently an old word for "dwelling." One characteristic feature, the *peristasis,* the row of columns surrounding the "house," may have its origin in wooden architecture; but Egyptian and Syrian ornamental elements were adopted too. The invention of ceramic tiles came to determine the characteristic slope of the pediment, first adopted at the temple of the Isthmian sanctuary toward 600 B.C.[51] This became the model for the temples that all major cities began to build soon after this date. And here too non-Greek neighbors were soon following the Greek example, notably the Etruscans and the Romans. In the appurtenances of the sanctuaries, water basins, lamps and incense, votive objects, halls and sacristies, the Near Eastern–Mediterranean *koine* persisted.

In the literary and spiritual fields the impact on Greece of Mesopotamia, Syria, Egypt, or Iran is less easy to determine. Much of it was probably lost without leaving a trace, whereas palpable objects are lacking. In the end, the Greek achievement is certainly unique, even if we are reluctant to speak of a Greek miracle.[52] It is difficult to assess which were the determining forces, the social and economic factors which must have invited and promoted the craftsmen's skills, the merchants' enterprise, and the Greek ways of language and thought. No doubt the Greek success had to do with freedom—of enterprise, of speech, of imagination, even of religion. The polycentricity of the Greek world must have played its role, the rise of the polis, the political system without a dominating and suffocating central power, the openness for agonistic competition, even if this meant a lack of stability. If the development of royal authority and state administration had been a necessary precondition for the establishment of high cultures in the East, their further development depended upon the retreat of the state and the opening of unlimited opportunity for small groups and individuals. This evidently was the case in Greece, especially in the enterprise of sea trade which, despite incalculable risks, did much to raise the general standard of living. Highly skilled craftsmen too were free individuals who migrated in search of jobs and recognition and could even attain citizenship in cities they had chosen to live in. It is characteristic that they began to sign their works with their proper names.[53] Greeks had mostly chased out their own kings or drastically reduced their power. Within small city states, sizable population groups were involved in politics, claiming autonomy. The tendency was toward legal equality of male citizens. Democracy was on its way.

It was also an old tradition that certain wise men emerged in a city as counselors of political friends or of larger civic groups; now even in this area individual competition took over, bringing conflict of opinion, discussion, rhetorical vigor, and fierce argumentation. Just as in politics, sentence clashed against sentence. The practice of discussion and argument would win in the end against the perpetuation of authority.[54]

No doubt Phoenician cities such as Tyre or Carthage had similar tendencies and opportunities,[55] as they had developed similar forms of economy. They too profited from the freedom and small-scale intensity available at the fringes of the great empires. Carthage, as the Greeks saw it, was endowed with a form of constitution, *politeia*. But even so, the city adopted and imported the Greek art style, and in the Hellenistic period philosophers traveled from Carthage—prior to its destruction in 146 B.C.—to Athens to make their career in Greek philosophy. What determined the shape of world civilization was Greek.

I

Alphabetic Writing

Among oriental imports in Greece, by far the most important was the alphabet. If modernization and democracy seem to be linked to literacy up to the present day, the Greeks were among the first to achieve such a state, thanks to their Eastern neighbors. For this reason the invention and diffusion of the alphabet must be outlined briefly here, even if this mainly means summing up what is generally known to scholarship.[1]

The Greeks said the alphabet was Phoenician, and there is no doubt about its Semitic origin. *Alpha* and *beta,* "ox" and "house," are current Semitic words; they do not make sense in Greek. Two arbitrary but significant items start a sequence to be remembered as the basis of a very special ability. Writing had developed in the old high cultures since the beginning of the third millennium; it had also been instrumental in developing them, be it in the form of Egyptian hieroglyphs or Mesopotamian cuneiform. Yet these old writing systems were so complicated, comprising hundreds of signs with multiple functions, that it required years of training and continuous practice to handle them with expertise. Hence the writers were the intellectuals, the learned community, limited in number but with unlimited prestige; "lords of the tablet" they called themselves in Mesopotamia. Syllabic scripts which were developed in the Bronze Age, such as Linear A and B in Crete and Mycenaean Greece, could do with about 80 signs, which was significant improvement, no doubt. But they still remained in the hands of the palatial bureaucracy, as far as we know, and mostly disappeared along with the palatial system in the great crisis of about 1200 B.C. The decisive advance was the discovery that you can record language with about 25 signs—phonemes, modern linguists would say. Such a system can be learned by any person of medium intelligence within a short period of time. We do not know the author of this decisive step nor the place of its invention, which must have occurred in the region of western Semites. Connections have been traced to Egyptian hieroglyphs and to the scarce Sinai inscriptions, which are difficult to interpret.[2] A derivative form, a transformation into cuneiform, was in use at Ugarit in the Late Bronze Age[3] and disappeared again. The real breakthrough came only after the crisis of the palaces. Unfortunately in this case, modernization meant the adoption of perishable writing materials, wooden tablets and leather scrolls instead of clay tablets; this caused documentation to disappear, except for graffiti.

The inventor had the brilliant idea not only to give names to his signs in an acrophonic system, but to organize them in a fixed sequence to be memorized like a comic sing-song, "ox, house, crook,[4] door," and so on; in Semitic this sounded something like "alpu betu gamlu daltu." The signs vaguely represent these objects, with radical simplification of drawing: a few strokes, or one curve or circle, will suffice for each sign. The Egyptians had eschewed such simplification for their hieroglyphs, whereas the clay impressions of cuneiform had produced quite different drawings.

Only a few or unclear documents of alphabetic writing antedate 1200 B.C., and there are very few for the next centuries.[5] It looks as if the vast diffusion occurred after the tenth century. The same script is used for Phoenician-Canaanite, Hebrew, and

Aramaic. The alphabet infiltrated even the center of cuneiform writing, the Assyrian empire. The "writers of scrolls," writing in Aramaic, appear side by side with the "lords of the tablets," even if these were successful in securing their privileges.[6] Darius, king of Persia, still deemed it necessary to have some kind of cuneiform for his Persian inscriptions, and so commissioned a new form of cuneiform; but this newly invented script was hardly used beyond official records. In any case the main document, the rock inscription of Bagastana-Behistun, could only be read by gods.[7] Elamic cuneiform, from the original home of Cyrus, was still kept in use for a few generations; for use in general administration, however, it was alphabetic Aramaic that gained the day and thus rose to the status of "imperial Aramaic."

The adoption of the alphabet by the Greeks occurred, as far as we can tell, shortly after 800 B.C. A linear writing system of Mycenaean type had survived at Cyprus. But the bulk of the Greeks decided to write "Phoenician." The Greeks carefully learned the names of the letters, *alpha, beta, gamma, delta,* pronouncing them in their own phonetics, and they kept to their immutable sequence. The letter forms, too, are practically identical at first. The place of takeover is unknown. Although the Greeks called the system Phoenician, this leaves open whether these were Phoenicians in our sense, people from Byblos, Tyre, and Sidon together with their colonies from Cyprus to Africa, or rather Aramaeans from north Syria. That the transfer took place at Cyprus is plausible;[8] the change between writing from right to left and writing from left to right would be understandable exactly there, since linear writing left to right was overcrossing with the Semitic import written right to left. But there are no documents so far for alphabetic writing from archaic Cyprus. The old documents for Greek writing follow the lines of commerce, as to be expected, from Al Mina in Syria to Euboea and to Ischia, not leaving out Naxos and Athens. The oldest letters so far come

from the region of Gabii close to Rome.[9] Some other documents
may still be attributed to the first half of the eighth century; then
a kind of explosion of writing took place in the second half of
that century. It seems that the new technique spread through the
whole of the Greek world within a few decades. Its success is also
evident in its rapid adoption by the neighboring peoples, the
Phrygians in the east and the Etruscans in the west, to be followed by Lydians and Lycians in Anatolia[10] and by Latini, Veneti,
and Iberi on the other side of the Mediterranean.

What has often been acclaimed as the first major contribution
of the Greeks to world civilizations is in fact a strange mixture of
misunderstanding and genius. In contrast to the Semites, the
Greeks regularly write vowels, as do their neighbors, from Phrygians to Etruscans and Latin tribes. Semites found this superflu-
ous: Arabs and Hebrews have retained the principle of consonant
script up to now. They still indicate long vowels, *a, i, u,* by the
signs of *aleph, waw,* and *jod.* The beginnings of this orthography
of vowels are now attested in Syria even before the Greek takeover.[11]

The progress of the Greeks mainly arose from misunderstanding.[12] As they were learning that old mnemonic sequence and understanding the acrophonic principle, *alpha,* in their ears and
minds, would start with *a,* not with a consonantal stop sign, and
jod, which they had to pronounce *iota,* would start with *i,* not
with *j,* which did not exist in their language; thus the main innovation was to make two signs out of *waw,* one for *w* and one for
u, later called *y-psilon,* and to place this vowel at the end of the series. That the letter *'ayin,* possibly pronounced *'en*—the word
means "eye," still clearly recognizable in the letter form *O*—was
to represent the vowel *o* may have been a systematic decision, un-
less there was some Semitic dialect to suggest this pronunciation.
Further differentiations were quickly elaborated by local dialects,
often with additional letters at the end of the series, as was also

done in Latin and much later in the Slavic versions. In principle, the sequence of ox-house/alpha-beta has persisted; our computers have long been taught to respect it.

Together with the alphabet the Greeks also adopted the writing tablet, which retained its Semitic name in Greek, *deltos,* and the leather scroll and the layout of books, with the characteristic *subscriptio,* the indication of title and scribe at the end of the text instead of a title at the beginning.[13]

The early advent of literature in its full sense in Greece is suggested by two famous and much-discussed verse inscriptions dated about 730 B.C., the Dipylon Inscription from Athens and the Nestor Cup from Ischia.[14] Especially the Nestor Cup with its careful writing—one verse, one line—hardly leaves doubt that whoever wrote it had seen books with Greek poetry by that time. Written documents of merchants dealing with long-distance trade exist from the sixth century in the form of letters written on lead;[15] wooden tablets, leather, and papyrus would have disintegrated over time. There is no doubt that professional poets and musicians could read and write after the seventh century; even the invention of musical notation may go back to the sixth century. Elementary school teaching is in evidence since about 500, and the introduction of *ostrakismos* in Athens by that time, a form of written vote, presupposes the general ability of writing and reading for every citizen, even if reality was to lag behind the project. A reading public evolved during the fifth century and was dominant after the fourth. Innovation and experiment have been grounded in books ever since.

2

Orientalizing Features in Homer

Homer and the Orient" is not a new pairing. At least since Hugo Grotius (1644), "Homer and the Old Testament" has been a field of persistent interest, partly carrying on the old controversy over whether Hebrew or Greek, Moses or Homer, was the older and more original starting point of literacy and culture. It was noticed that Isaiah (31.4) has a beautiful lion simile comparable to Homer's similes, and that Jahweh takes his oath by Heaven and Earth (Deuteronomy 4.26) just like Homer's Hera (*Iliad* 15.36). The sacrifices of Iphigenia and of Jephtha's daughter were found to be parallel, even as a subject for operas. Historians also called attention to the Phoenicians and the Egyptians, who loom large in Homer's *Odyssey.*[1]

The break, the isolation of the Hellenic paradigm, came with the beginning of the nineteenth century.[2] Yet by then the discoveries from Egypt and Mesopotamia had gradually grown in importance. In 1872 the news about a Babylonian Story of the Flood caused sensation; these were tablets X–XI of *Gilgamesh.* About the same time the Egyptian texts about the battle of Qadesh were translated, which present the king in combat very much like a Homeric hero, with chariots and with gods intervening in battle;[3] these were joined by the texts about the Sea Peoples from about

1200 B.C., with the names of Achaeans, Dardanoi, Philistines, and Teukroi.[4] In 1884 the first edition of *Gilgamesh* appeared, as well as *Ishtar's Descent,* with the impressive German title *Ischtars Höllenfahrt* (Descent into Hell).[5]

Yet Gilgamesh was first presented to the public under the name of *Izdubar;* see *Roschers Mythologisches Lexikon* or Hermann Usener's *Sintfluthsagen* (1899);[6] his friend Enkidu was read as *Eabani* at that time. Students of cuneiform know about such multiple readings of cuneiform signs; for outsiders, including classicists, this must be confusing and anything but trust-inspiring. The ancient Orient was to remain exotic. In consequence, "Homer and the Orient" remained a domain for outsiders. William Ewart Gladstone (1809–1898), better known in his role as British Prime Minister, called attention to the Egyptian texts about the Sea Peoples, and he was the first to compare Oceanus and Tethys in Homer's *Iliad* with Apsu and Tiamat at the beginning of the Babylonian epic of creation, *Enuma Elish.*[7] Classicists shook their heads in indignation. The exaggerated claims of some orientalists about *Gilgamesh* and world literature—Peter Jensen, Hugo Winckler, Adolf Jeremias—were rather counterproductive. Few read Carl Fries, *Das Zagmukfest auf Scheria* (1910), which took its title from Sumerian to interpret the *Odyssey* as a ritual drama.[8] More sober were Hermann Wirth, *Homer und Babylon* (1921), and Arthur Ungnad, *Gilgamesch-Epos und Odyssee* (1923), but their books were anything but a success. Ungnad did not even find a publisher; his book was self-published.[9]

Nevertheless some striking observations about the Orient and Homer come from these studies at the beginning of the twentieth century, such as the comparison of Gilgamesh's voyage to Utnapishtim with motifs found in the *Odyssey,* or of the appearance of Enkidu's ghost to Gilgamesh, so like the *psyche* of Patroklos appearing to Achilles; even a skeptic like G. S. Kirk found this parallel "almost irresistible."[10]

In the following pages comparisons with Mesopotamian literature will be prominent. This seems to be a far step from Greece. Yet cuneiform literature is the biggest corpus of ancient oriental literature, much richer than Hittite, let alone Ugaritic, more variegated even than Egyptian, whereas no literary text in Mycenaean Linear B has thus far been discovered. The cuneiform corpus is also outstanding for its truly sophisticated level. It was transmitted through centuries, indeed millennia, by the tradition of the scribal schools, the "houses of tablets," so that older classics competed with more modern pieces. But above all, contacts of all sorts were continuous. Cuneiform dominates Bronze Age Syria, and when it gave way to the alphabet there after 1200, Assyrians came into direct contact with the Greeks all the more. This interaction had its apogee in the eighth and seventh centuries, which of course does not exclude earlier contacts in Syria and Cyprus. Still, the later encounters and frictions are documented in a much fuller way.[11] The most significant import, alphabetic writing, had come to the Greeks already at the beginning of the Assyrian period.[12] Yet since the writing materials used in the new technique were perishable, in contrast to the clay tablets of cuneiform, the direct evidence for oriental literature in Syria and beyond disappeared at the very moment when it reached the Greeks.[13] This gap was to persist.

In a certain sense the Greek epic of Homeric style may be regarded as a very self-dependent flowering. The formulaic system, which Milman Parry has discovered and explained as an essential function within an oral tradition, is tied to the Greek language. From this point of view Homer has become the model example of an oral tradition.[14] By contrast, the Eastern epics, at least in Mesopotamia, are based upon a fixed tradition of writing and schools of scribes, spanning more than two thousand years. Tablets were copied and recopied again and again, sometimes also translated into other cuneiform languages. Epics were used as school texts; only indirect clues indicate oral performance.

Hence one might expect to encounter quite different princi-

ples of style and structure in the East and in the West. Yet whoever cares to take account of both sides will be struck by the similarities. They had been noted for a long time. Cecil Maurice
Bowra, in his *Heroic Poetry,* consistently refers to *Gilgamesh.* The
similarities can be briefly summarized.[15] In both cases, in Greek
as in Akkadian, "epic" means narrative poetry which employs a
long verse repeated indefinitely, without strophic division; the
tale is about gods, sons of gods, and great men from the past, all
of whom may interact with each other. Main characteristics of
style are the standard epithets, the formulaic verses, the repetition
of verses, and typical scenes such as the "assembly of the gods."

Epithets have always appeared to be a special characteristic of
Homeric style, a feature that affects translations. We are familiar
with "cloud-gathering Zeus," "Odysseus of many counsels," and
"rosy-fingered Dawn." In Akkadian and Ugaritic epic too the
chief characters have their own epithets.[16] The chief god, Enlil,
often appears as "the hero Enlil," the hero of the flood is
"Utnapishtim the far-away," and the dangerous "Seven" in the
Erra epic are "champions without peer." Similarly, the Ugaritic
epics have fixed formulas such as "the Virgin Anat" or "Danel the
Rephaite." What sounds even more Homeric is a warrior "knowl-
edgeable in battle"; it is less clear why the Mistress of the Gods
is "good at shouting," but it was equally unclear to Greeks why
Calypso as well as Circe should be "a frightful goddess using
speech," *deine theos audeessa.* Be that as it may, epithets must be
there. The earth is "the broad earth," and a god of heavens is "father of gods and men." The epithets are decorative insofar as they
are not essential for the actual context or the given situation, nor
specially modeled for it. They are, however, extremely helpful
when the poet needs to fill out a verse line.

What is most striking about formulaic verse is the complicated
introduction of direct speech. The lavish use of direct speech, the
representation of whole scenes in the form of dialogue, is indeed

a peculiarity of the genre. In Akkadian, the introductory formula is, in literal translation: "He set his mouth and spoke, to . . . he said (the word)."[17] The simple meaning of "speak" is expressed in three synonyms. It is the same with the well-known Homeric formula: "He raised his voice and spoke the winged words." It is perhaps even more remarkable that characters, reflecting on a new situation, may "speak to their own heart." "Consulting with her heart she spoke, indeed she took counsel with herself"—so Siduri in *Gilgamesh;* direct speech follows.[18] In a similar way Homeric heroes speak to their own "great-hearted *thymos*" or to their "heart." When Gilgamesh does his traveling, the new day is always introduced with the same formula: "Barely a shimmer of the morning dawned,"[19] not identical but still reminiscent of Homer's famous line, "But when early-born rosy-fingered Dawn appeared." It is natural for a narrative to move from day to day, but to employ stereotyped formulas for sunset and sunrise, pause and action, is a specific technique used in *Gilgamesh* as in Homer.

Among the repetitions which cover a whole sequence of verses a striking feature is the exact verbal correspondence between command and performance, reporting and repetition of the report. The Mesopotamian scribes, weary of their wedges, occasionally used a repeat sign, which the Homeric scribes did not permit themselves.

Among typical scenes the assembly of the gods is prominent. In Akkadian this is a fixed concept *(puhur ilani);* the expression is the same in Ugaritic, and an analogous scene is also fully elaborated in the Hittite *Song of Ullikummi.*[20] The assembly of gods is also found in the Hebrew Bible.[21] One might say that the oriental assembly of the gods is more a kind of senate, whereas Homer introduces a family, including current family catastrophes such as mutual scolding of parents and blows for the children. Frequently, the assembly of the gods decides to send out a messenger.

Comparisons are a popular device in Akkadian epic as in related poetry; lions are favorite similes.[22] One remarkable feature, at least in *Gilgamesh,* the longest and most artful text, is that more complicated forms of narrative technique are tried out, and these also appear in the *Odyssey.* In the eleventh tablet of *Gilgamesh* a distant but particularly gripping piece of action, the great flood, is incorporated in the form of direct speech, as a tale by the main participant, Utnapishtim "the far-away," in a first-person narration. The double action at the beginning of the *Gilgamesh* epic is neatly constructed to bring together the main characters, Enkidu and Gilgamesh; the narrative first follows Enkidu's adventures and his transformation from savage to civilized by means of sex, and only then brings in Gilgamesh and his preparations for the encounter through direct speech of the prostitute, addressing Enkidu.[23] Thus even the narrative technique of the poet of the *Odyssey* has a kind of model. The *Odyssey* incorporates most of Odysseus' adventures in first-person narrative, an account by Odysseus himself at the Phaeacians' palace; the story also engineers a double plot to bring Telemachus and Odysseus together. The similarity between the openings of *Gilgamesh* and the *Odyssey* has also struck readers: attention is called to a hero who wandered wide and saw many things—while his name is intentionally withheld.[24]

Foreshadowing the *Iliad,* as it were, *Gilgamesh* exhibits a certain ethos of the mortality of humans. The main theme of the poem, in its own words, is the fate of humanity *(shimatu awilutim),* which means death, in contrast to the enduring life of the gods. Only Utnapishtim succeeds in winning such a life for himself; Gilgamesh is bound to fail. Before his fight with Humbaba, the demon of the woods, Gilgamesh draws the heroic consequence: "The gods, with Shamash (the sun god) they sit forever; as for mankind, numbered are their days . . . But you here, you fear death? . . . I will go ahead of you . . . If I myself were to fall, let me still set up my name."[25] Thus, precisely because man is denied eternal life, it remains for him to win fame at the risk of death, fame which will survive as a "name, set up" forever. In the *Iliad*, a leading concept is that of "imperishable glory" *(kleos aphthiton)*, in contrast to "mortal men." "Yes, dear friend! If, having escaped from this war, we were to live forever, ageless, immortal, even I would not fight among the front ranks . . . But now, as the demons of death stand before us anyhow . . . Let us go, whether we bring glory to another man or someone gives glory to us"—this is Homer.[26] Such an insight into the limits of the human condition does not, however, lead to caution in the face of the gods. Aggressive outbursts against them do occur. Enkidu throws the hind leg of the bull of heaven to Ishtar and shouts: "If I caught you, like to this I would do to you." "Indeed I would take revenge if I only had the power," cries Achilles to Apollo when the god has deceived him.[27]

Closer comparisons could also be made between the actual battle scenes of East and West. One notable example of combat poetry is the Egyptian text about pharaoh Ramses II in the battle of Qadesh. The hero all of a sudden finds himself alone amidst the enemies and prays to his father, the god Amun. The god hears him, he speaks words of encouragement, whereupon Ramses attacks and kills all the enemies in his onslaught.[28] Another suggestive text is incorporated in the Annals of Sennacherib. It refers to the battle of Halule in 691 B.C. and presents the king's combat in a nearly Homeric style, starting with the king as he takes up his armor piece by piece, mounts his chariot, and charges into battle to defeat the enemies, with the assistance of his god: "My prancing steeds, harnessed for riding, plunged into the streams of blood as into a river; the wheels of my chariot, which brings down the wicked and the evil, were bespattered with blood and filth." Note the ornamental characterizations of horses and chariot. The Assyrian king is fighting from his Bronze

Age chariot, just like Ramses the Egyptian. We are irresistibly reminded of the *Iliad:* "Thus under great-hearted Achilles his
single-hoofed horses stepped on corpses and shields alike; with
blood the whole axle was bespattered, and the rails around the
seat, which the drops from the hoofs of the horses were hitting."[29]
Considering the date of the Assyrian text, one might even toy
with the idea that some Greek singer had been present among
Greek mercenaries and composed such a song on the battle of
Halule, which so much pleased the king that it was incorporated
into the official annals, where it makes strange contrast with the
usual dreary and dull listings of killing and plundering. But more
systematic research into the genre of combat descriptions is
needed. The Song of Deborah and Barak in the Hebrew Bible
should not be forgotten in this context; it has, among other stir-
ring events, a remarkable battle at the river.[30]

Some further connections in detail between East and West,
though striking, have remained a mystery. This applies to the saying of "Tree and Stone" as it appears at Ugarit, in Jeremiah, and
in Homer and Hesiod. The expression seems to be connected to a
myth about the origin of man in the Hebrew Bible and in the
Odyssey, but is used rather as a worn-out commonplace at Ugarit
as in the *Iliad* and in Hesiod.[31]

It is less surprising that the blessing of the land under the rule
of a good king, as we find it in Homer and Hesiod, appears all
the more in Mesopotamia. The earth brings her crops, the trees
grow their fruit, the animals thrive, and "people thrive under
him" (the good king)—this is Odysseus addressing Penelope, or
Hesiod praising the goddess of Justice (Dike). But this is also
Assurbanipal speaking about himself: "Since the gods . . . be-
nignly made me take my seat on the throne of my father, my begetter, Adad, released his torrents of rain, Ea opened his springs,
the ears of the crops grew five ells high . . . the fruits of the field
flourished . . . the trees brought their fruits to an abundant

growth, the cattle bred successfully. During my reign there was abundance, during my years good things overflowed."[32]

Bringing together similar motifs, as has been done here, might, of course, bring to mind the application of rhyming etymologies. They are baffling, sometimes impressive, and usually inconclusive. Approximately the same will be found everywhere. Yet side by side with individual motifs more complex structures appear, and in such cases sheer coincidence is much less likely. Thus we find a system of major deities and a basic cosmological idea; decrees of the gods to decimate mankind, which has become a burden to the earth; the narrative structure of a family scene among gods with appropriate characters. It should also be clear that once the historical link, the fact of transmission, has been established in a single case, the dam is broken. Further connections, including linguistic borrowings, become more and more likely, although these alone would hardly suffice to carry the burden of proof.

Some passages in the *Iliad*, all at the level of the divine scenery, show close correspondences to important passages in the most important Akkadian epics: *Atrahasis, Gilgamesh,* and *Enuma Elish.* To begin with, take Gladstone's observation about Oceanus and Tethys (n. 7). This concerns the section of the *Iliad* which the ancients called the Deception of Zeus *(Dios Apate).* Its peculiarities have been commented upon in Homeric studies; Albrecht Dihle, listing linguistic peculiarities, found so many deviations from the normal traditional use of Homeric formulas that he came up with the thesis that this section of the *Iliad* could not belong to the phase of oral tradition, but must be a written composition.[33] This has not been generally accepted, but it should be acknowledged that we are dealing here with a text which is unusual for its linguistics and content. It is modern in a way, it must have its special prehistory. One peculiarity of content stands out which already struck Plato and Aristotle, and possibly some

Presocratics even before Plato: this is the only passage in the Homeric compositions where cosmogony unexpectedly comes to the fore. Aristotle, for one, found here the very beginning of natural philosophy, the possible inspiration for Thales.[34] In the passage in question Hera says that she is going to Oceanus, "origin of the gods," and Tethys the "mother"; later on Oceanus is even called "the origin of all." Oceanus and Tethys, the primeval couple, Hera alleges, have withheld their nuptial rights from one another for a long time, separated as a result of strife, *neikea*.[35] This sounds like an anticipation of the Empedoclean *Neikos* cosmogony. The genesis of the gods, who once originated from Oceanus and Tethys, has come to an end. It is true that within the *Iliad* narrative this account is all made up by Hera; it is a patent lie. But the motifs of myth that come up here are not invented; they even radiate beyond those speeches. The very climax of this song, when Zeus and Hera make love on the summit of Mount Ida within a golden cloud, from which resplendent drops are falling, shows divinity in a naturalistic setting which is not otherwise a feature of Homeric anthropomorphism. The division of the cosmos into three parts split among the major gods, told in Poseidon's later speech,[36] is the third motif here, which brings the gods to bear on the origin and function of our natural cosmos. All of this is unique in Homer, to be found just in this passage.

Oceanus and Tethys, "origin" and "mother," have a parallel in the Babylonian epic *Enuma Elish*.[37] "When above," this text begins, "skies were not yet named nor earth below pronounced by name, Apsu, the first, their begetter, and Tiamat, who bore them all, had mixed their waters together . . . then gods were born within them." Snakes came first, then proper gods who are venerated in cult. Apsu means ground water, Tiamat is the Sea; mixing together, begetter and mother, they were there first, and the origin of all. Mixing and birth, though, came to an end later when Ea put Apsu to sleep and killed him, and Marduk, in a dramatic fight, overcame Tiamat, who had become dangerous and destructive. Then Marduk established the cosmos as it is standing now.

Certainly Hera's inventions correspond to the beginning of *Enuma Elish* to a surprising degree. Apsu and Tiamat equal Oceanus and Tethys as the original parental couple. But Tethys was not at all an active figure in Greek mythology. In contrast to the sea goddess Thetis, mother of Achilles—with whom she was sometimes confused even in antiquity—Tethys had no established cults; and no one knew anything further to tell about her.[38] She seems to exist only by virtue of the Homeric passage; how she came to rank as the primeval mother nobody knew in Greece. Here the rhyming of the names comes into play. *Ti-amat* is the form normally written in the cuneiform text of *Enuma Elish*. The normal form of the basic Akkadian word, however, is *tiamtu* or *tâmtu*, the word for "sea." The name can be written in this more phonetic orthography; but in the texts of *Enuma Elish* we also find it in the form of *taw(a)tu*. And we can see how Tawtu would become Tethys in Greek, with the sound of "w" disappearing, and long *a* changing to long *e* in Ionian.[39] The different dentals in this transcription, *t* and *th,* follow the normal sequence of Greek orthography. Sophilos the vase painter wrote ΘΕΘΤΣ.[40] When the text of *Enuma Elish* became known to Eudemus, the pupil of Aristotle, he rendered the name as Tauthe.[41] This seems to reproduce *Tawtu* (with case forms *Tawti, Tawta*). The change of the long vowel *a* to *e* in the Ionian dialect has parallels in other comparatively recent borrowings, such as *Kubaba* becoming *Kybebe, Baal* becoming *Belos,* and *Mada* known as *Medes (Medoi).* Thus the argument seems valid that here, right in the middle of the *Iliad,* the mysterious name of the primeval mother comes directly from an Akkadian classic and thus bears witness to its influence.

Note that there can be no question of Bronze Age borrowing in this case. Four hundred years of oral tradition in Greece would have led to stronger distortions in the process of assimilation; it is even not at all clear whether the *Enuma Elish* is old enough for Bronze Age transfer.[42] This confirms from the other side Albrecht Dihle's observations on the late character of this Homeric piece. We are dealing, in the words of Martin West, with a "neo-oriental element."

Once an oriental background is established in the Deception of Zeus, further observations are bound to follow. Aphrodite has clear but complex connections with the East.[43] The embroidered girdle *(kestos)* Hera borrowed from Aphrodite as a love charm seems to have special Eastern characteristics.[44] The catalogue of women once loved by Zeus, which the god lists in his speech to Hera—condemned by ancient critics—has its counterpart in Gilgamesh's enumeration of the lovers of Ishtar.[45] The oath of the gods which Hera is made to swear, ending "by the River Styx," is in fact a cosmic oath, binding together heaven, earth, and the waters of the underworld. It is precisely such a cosmic formula which concludes the enumeration of divine witnesses in the only Aramaic treaty text which has survived from the eighth century, the inscriptions from Sfire: "Heaven and earth, the deep and the springs, day and night."[46]

When Zeus the weather god makes love to his wife in a cloud on the top of the mountain, one recalls the image of the weather god and his unveiled wife poised upon their storm dragons, a theme very common in Near Eastern seal art; in addition, the marriage of heaven and earth is a mythical motif explicitly adduced in Akkadian literature.[47] A famous wooden statuette from the Heraion of Samos, of Zeus embracing Hera, is iconographically dependent on Eastern prototypes, even if its direct inspiration may come just from the text of the *Iliad*.[48]

More specific is the problem of Titans. Out of five Homeric passages in which the Titans—the old gods held prisoner in the underworld—are mentioned, three come from the context of the

Deception of Zeus. The other two are also in the context of divine scenes: proclamations of Zeus, father of the gods, to underline his sovereignty.[49] Since the discovery of the Kumarbi text it has been known that the Greeks share the concept of ancient, vanquished gods in the netherworld with Hittite, Phoenician, and Babylonian mythology. Details are complicated in the Greek as well as in the Eastern setting, as different traditions seem to merge. In Greek mythology the concept of the Titans as a collective group is not easily reconciled with the very special personality of Kronos, father of Zeus; conversely, the Hittite world view contains ancient gods in general, always mentioned collectively in the plural, in addition to Kumarbi, the hero of the Hurrian-Hittite succession myth. We learn that the weather god—who corresponds to Zeus—banished them to the netherworld. Corresponding deities in Mesopotamia are the "defeated" or "fettered gods," *ilani kamûti*. They too have been banished beneath the earth by the victorious god or gods. In the *Enuma Elish* these had been the supporters of Tiamat.[50] In other texts they are the Evil Seven who have been bound by the god of the heavens. Note that in Orphic tradition the Titans, sons of Heaven and Earth but "bound" in the netherworld, number exactly seven.[51]

The Evil Seven are especially prominent in the realm of exorcism and protective magic. This leads to a further possible connection: in protective magic, figurines are often fabricated for a ceremony and meant to be destroyed in the action. The most common material for this is clay, Akkadian *titu*. This word reached Greek, in the context of building technique, as *titanos*, plaster.[52] Later Greek authors have taken precisely this word to provide an etymology for the name of the Titans. When the Titans attacked the child Dionysus, they disguised their faces with plaster; hence their name. Although this etymology fails in the Greek language because the *i* of *Titanes/Titenes* is long whereas that of *titanos* is short, the Semitic word does have a long *i*, so that the hypothesis of borrowing brings back the ancient etymology. A ritual context can easily be imagined: the Titans bear their name as *tit* people because Eastern magicians used to fabricate clay figures—*ṣalme ṭiṭ* in Akkadian—to represent the defeated gods; such figures were used in protective magic and also as witnesses in oaths. This daring hypothesis still lacks evidence for verification; but even possibilities suggest context.

The connection of the *Dios Apate* with Akkadian literature became much closer with the publication of one of the oldest and most original Akkadian epics in 1969: *Atrahasis*. Small unpromising fragments had been known before.[53] The first version in three books is dated to the time of Ammiṣaduqa, a few generations after Hammurabi, in the seventeenth century B.C. Various old Babylonian tablets have survived in fragmentary form; the library of Assurbanipal contained several editions, with slight variants. A fragment of another recension has been found at Ugarit. This is a popular text which had been in circulation for more than a thousand years, a text which is astonishingly original and modern in its concept.

Atrahasis, the name we use for the title, means "outstanding by wisdom"; it would be more pertinent to speak of a Story of Mankind, as has been proposed. It begins with the paradoxical primordial situation "when gods were in the ways of men," with no humans yet in existence. Hence the gods had to do all the necessary work themselves, digging canals and building dikes. This led to a strike of the younger gods against their seniors, especially Enlil the acting chief. Fortunately, Enki the cunning god found a solution to the conflict. Together with the Mother Goddess he created men to act as robots instead of the gods, and to do all the work: henceforth "They shall bear the burden."

But soon, "after 600 (and?) 600 years," these creatures became too numerous, a real nuisance. The earth cries out, the gods are disturbed by their noise, so they try to annihilate their robots again. Three attempts are made at stereotyped intervals of 1200 years: first there is a plague, then a famine, and finally the flood. However, the cunning god of the deep, Enki, in alliance with the man "outstanding by wisdom," Atrahasis, frustrates the plans of destruction. He plays off the gods one against the other and before the flood tells Atrahasis to build his ark. The final part of the text, as can now be seen, is an older parallel version, probably the direct model, of *Gilgamesh* XI, the famous story of the flood which has been known since the nineteenth century. No doubt it influenced the story of Noah in the book of Genesis. The *Atrahasis,* however, is anything but an example of biblical piety; it views the gods in a critical way and is imbued with a remarkably human and slightly cynical optimism: whether the gods are with mankind or against it, humans are indestructible despite all their tribulations and afflictions. "How did man survive in the destruction?" Enlil, the leading god, slightly baffled, asks in the end as he perceives the ark upon the waters.[54] Yet mankind did survive.

At the beginning of the *Atrahasis* text, the Babylonian pantheon is introduced in a systematic fashion: "Anu, their father, was king; their counsellor was the warrior Enlil; their chamberlain was Ninurta; and their sheriff Ennugi." These verses are copied in the *Gilgamesh* epic, but not the following lines: "They grasped the flask of lots by the neck, they cast the lots; the gods made the division: Anu went up to heaven," a second god—there is a gap in the text here—"took the earth, for his subjects," and "the bolts, the bar of the sea, were set for Enki, the far-sighted." Enlil, the most active of the gods, must have been mentioned in the gap, to produce the usual trinity of Anu, Enlil, and Enki, sky god, weather god, water god. The *Atrahasis* text repeatedly comes back to this threefold division of the cosmos and the respective gods, particularly when Enlil tries to engineer a total blockade of the human world in order to enforce the famine.[55] A different version, tablet X,[56] has Anu and Adad (sky god and weather god) for the heavens and Sin and Nergal (moon god and god of the netherworld) for the earth; the realm of Enki, the Lord of the Deep, remains unchanged. The Deep does not mean the salted sea, but the potable ground waters and spring waters, which are also the realm of Poseidon in Greece, notwithstanding his power to rule the sea. Earth is made to include the underworld.

In the oft-quoted verses of the *Iliad,* the world is divided among the appropriate Homeric gods. Poseidon says: "For when we threw the lots I received the grey sea as my permanent abode, Hades drew the murky darkness, Zeus however drew the wide sky of brightness and clouds; the earth is common to all, and spacious Olympus."[57] This differs from the system of *Atrahasis* in that the earth together with the gods' mountain is declared to be a joint dominion; in the context of the story and on these grounds Poseidon insists on his right to become active in the battle on the plain of Troy. Yet the basic structure of both texts is astonishingly similar. There are three distinct areas of the cosmos—heaven, the depths of the earth, and the waters—and these three areas are assigned to the three major gods of the pantheon, male gods in every case. And in both instances the division is claimed to have been made by a mythical act, the gods drawing lots. This is not the normal practice among Greek gods: according to Hesiod, the other gods together asked Zeus to become their king when he had forcibly dethroned his predecessor—who was his father.[58] Also, from another point of view, this passage is unique in Greek epic: elsewhere, when the parts of the cosmos are enumerated, there is either a triad of heaven-earth-underworld or of heaven-sea-earth, or even heaven-earth-sea-underworld, but not the triad heaven-sea-underworld, which is here assigned to the three brothers. Furthermore, the three sons of Kronos and their realms do not have any further common part to play in Homer; nor do they make a triad in Greek cult. By contrast, in *Atrahasis* the pertinent passage is fundamental for the narrative and is referred to repeatedly.

No other passage in Homer comes so close to being a translation of the Akkadian epic. Actually, it is not really a translation but a resetting, yet in a way that shows the foreign framework. One might still believe this to be a deceptive coincidence, were it not for the special context of *Dios Apate* where many different clues come together to point to the oriental tradition; in this case, the coincidence hypothesis becomes the most improbable option.

In dealing with *Atrahasis* we cannot fail to perceive another important connection, which goes beyond the *Iliad*. The basic idea of this ancient Babylonian epic has a disconcertingly modern aspect: humans multiply, the earth feels oppressed by their actions; this must lead to catastrophe, to the annihilation of mankind. Yet mankind so far has survived all the threats or attempts of destruction; to secure the future, according to *Atrahasis,* only one means is left: birth control.[59] The birth control method suggested in the text, though, sounds less modern: it consists in the institution of priestesses who are not allowed to bear children.

The tribulation of earth is expressed in verses which recur at the beginning of each new act of *Atrahasis:* "Twelve hundred years had not yet passed, when the land extended and the peoples multiplied. The land was bellowing like a bull. The gods got disturbed with their uproar. Enlil heard their noise and he addressed the great gods: 'The noise of mankind has become too intense for me, with their uproar I am deprived of sleep.'" Hence Enlil proceeds to organize the catastrophes of plague, famine, and flood.[60]

This cannot be separated from a passage of Greek epic, an extremely prominent text in fact, the very beginning of the Trojan Cycle and the ultimate explanation of the cause of the Trojan War. This is the opening of the *Cypria,* an epic that was popular down to the classical epoch but fell into disregard and got lost afterwards. Already Herodotus doubted that Homer was the author,[61] though Pindar had taken it for granted. The opening lines of the *Cypria* have been preserved, albeit in a corrupt textual form, as a fragment, quoted to explain the "decision of Zeus" mentioned right at the beginning of the *Iliad* (1.5).

It all begins in the style of a fairy tale:[62]

> Once upon a time, when countless people moved on the face
>   of the earth. . .
> [gap; they oppressed?] the breadth of the deep-chested earth.
> Zeus saw this and took pity and deep in his heart
> He decided to relieve the all-nourishing earth of men
> By setting alight the great conflict of the Trojan War.

In the same commentary there is also a prose narrative:[63] "Earth, being oppressed by the multitude of men, since there was no piety among men, asked Zeus to be lightened of this burden. And first Zeus caused at once the Theban War by which he thoroughly destroyed many men. Afterwards again he caused the Trojan War, consulting with Momos—this is called 'the decision of Zeus' by Homer—he could have destroyed them all with lightnings or floods, but Momos prevented this and suggested rather two measures to him, to marry Thetis to a human and to generate a beautiful daughter." Thus eventually Achilles and Helen are born and with them the principal actors of the Trojan War.

The two texts cannot be combined directly. In the verses quoted, Zeus reacts to the conditions on earth, seeing and feeling pity with her plight, and he immediately plans the Trojan War. As the excerpts from the *Cypria* in Proclos indicate, Zeus discussed further details with Themis.[64] In the prose version, however, the earth is not a dumb object of pity, but a speaking partner. The decision first leads to the Theban War; this is followed by a strange discussion with Momos. We are clearly dealing with two competing versions. In fact a third version comes from the end of the Hesiodic *Catalogues*.[65] Here Zeus alone makes his decision, which the others "did not yet fully comprehend." His aim is to bring an end to the confusion of human and divine spheres, and thereby to bring the age of heroes to a close. "He sought to destroy the greater part of mankind" through the catastrophe of war. According to Hesiod's *Works and Days* (163–5), it was both the Theban and the Trojan wars that brought the end of the age of heroes. It is true that the text of the *Catalogues* is so badly preserved in this section that it is not fully comprehensible, but this much is clear: the catastrophe is linked to Helen.

Thus we have three variations of the basic concept of a catastrophe of mankind, wrought by the decision of the ruling god. Both the *Cypria* and the *Catalogues,* even if we cannot give them an exact dating, must belong to the archaic period; the source of the prose version cannot be fixed in time. Yet it is precisely the prose version which has a particular affinity with the *Atrahasis* text. Here plans for different catastrophes, while not acted out, are still considered in a systematic fashion, and somewhat surprisingly, it is the flood which appears as the most radical measure. What is particularly strange is the role of Momos, the personification of Reproach, as it seems; in an awkward poetic strategy he is introduced only here as an advisor of Zeus just to rebuke two suggestions. Or is it his role to reproach mankind? What is even more interesting is that, at the beginning of *Enuma Elish*, Apsu, the "the first one, the begetter," distressed by the noise of the younger gods who are depriving him of his sleep, makes plans to kill them all, and while planning this he has an advisor at his side, *Mummu,* "giving counsel to Apsu."[66] Is Momos the same as Mummu? If so, the Greek text would present a contamination of motifs from *Atrahasis* and *Enuma Elish*—as appears to be the case in the context of the Deception of Zeus too. This still does not permit placing the Greek prose text securely within the framework of Greek literature. But the possibility of a close Eastern connection gains strength from a similar case: for the figure of the Greek monster Typhon-Typhoeus, a prose text preserved in the library of Apollodorus provides the most striking parallel to the Hittite myth of Illuyankas the dragon; the text itself may have a Hellenistic source.[67]

As regards the *Cypria,* the *Atrahasis* text proves at any rate that the motif of the oppression of the earth and the plan of the destruction of mankind by the highest god, the weather god, is extremely old.[68] This must give pause to those who find sheer post-Homeric invention in the opening of the *Cypria.* In fact there is a further reference to the East even from the title: *Cypria* can only refer to the island of Cyprus, however skeptical we may be about the later information that named Stasinus of Cyprus as the author of the poem. That the story told in *Cypria* was known around 650 B.C. is indicated by the representation of the Judgment of Paris on the Chigi vase,[69] beside the verses about Paris' decision in the twenty-fourth book of the *Iliad,* a highly disputed passage.[70] The vase would point to that epoch when Cyprus, though rich and powerful, was formally under Assyrian sovereignty. That period on Cyprus appears to be characterized by a mixture of Eastern luxury and Homeric lifestyle. The burials are as lavish as that of Patroclus; there is elaborate Eastern furniture; horses are sacrificed and interred in the chamber tombs together with the chariots; even a "sword with silver nails," as known from Homeric diction, has been found. This does not explain why the Homeric theme of the Trojan War caught the imagination of Cypriots, but a "Cyprian epic" is a fact, as are the memorial steles of Assyrian kings in the cities of Cyprus.[71]

The "apparatus of the gods" which accompanies the events narrated in the *Iliad* and, in a modified form, in the *Odyssey,* has more than once been called a late element in the tradition of Greek heroic epic. It is here that oriental parallels stand out. Granted, the double stage of divine and human actions, which is handled in such a masterful way by the composer of the *Iliad*, is not found in this systematic form in the Mesopotamian epics.[72] Still, *Atrahasis* and *Gilgamesh* too repeatedly introduce the gods interacting with the deeds and sufferings of men; and Eastern kings boast that they have won their heroic fights in direct contact with their protective gods.

Gilgamesh features one famous encounter of divinity and man. When Gilgamesh has killed Humbaba, the demon of the forest, and has cleansed himself of the grime of battle, Ishtar "raised an eye at the beauty of Gilgamesh": "Do but grant me of your fruit!" she says, and she offers fabulous goods to him. But Gilgamesh scornfully rejects her, giving a catalogue of all her partners whom she once "has loved" only to destroy or to transform them. "If you would love me, you would [treat me] like them." Whereupon

> Ishtar, when hearing this,
> Ishtar was enraged and [went up] to the heaven.
> Forth went Ishtar before Anu, her father;
> Before Antum, her mother her tears were flowing:
> "Oh my father! Gilgamesh has heaped insults upon me!
> Gilgamesh has recounted my insults,
> My insults and my curses."
> Anu opened his mouth to speak,
> He said to glorious Ishtar:
> "Surely you have provoked King Gilgamesh,
> And [thus] Gilgamesh recounted your insults,
> Your insults and your curses.[73]

Compare a scene from the *Iliad*. While trying to protect Aeneas, her son, Aphrodite has been wounded by Diomedes. Her blood is flowing. "But she, beside herself, went away, she felt horrible pain." With the help of Iris and Ares she reached Olympus.

"But she, glorious Aphrodite, fell into the lap of Dione, her mother; she took her daughter in her arms, stroked her with her hand, spoke the word and said: 'Who has done such things to you, dear child?'" Aphrodite replies: "the son of Tydeus, high-minded Diomedes, has wounded me." Mother sets out to comfort her with mythical examples about other gods who had to suffer pain. Her sister Athena, less kind, makes a scornful comment—she is on the other side, she has been assisting Diomedes. But Zeus, her father, smiles. "He called golden Aphrodite and said to her: 'My child, you are not given the works of war! But you should pursue the tender offices of marriage.'" In other words, it's partly your own fault.[74]

The two scenes are parallel to one another in structure, narrative form, and ethos to an astonishing degree. A goddess, injured by a human, goes up to heaven to complain to her father and her mother, and she earns a mild rebuke from her father. Of course this may be called a universal scenario from the realm of children's stories. The scene repeats itself with variations in the battle of the gods later in the *Iliad:* Artemis, after being beaten by Hera, climbs to the knees of father Zeus, weeping. He draws her to himself and asks, laughing: "Who did this to you?" She replies: "Your wife beat me."[75] The scene from the Diomedes book is simpler in that both parents appear as a refuge, the stepmother being left out, with the father taking the stance of slightly distanced superiority. This corresponds exactly to the *Gilgamesh* scene.

But what is more, the persons involved in both scenes are likewise identical: the sky god, his wife, and their daughter, the goddess of love. Aphrodite in general is the equivalent of Ishtar;[76] she has offered herself to a mortal man, Anchises the father of Aeneas, and Anchises suffered a strange fate as a result of his contact with the goddess[77]—this would be another case of what Gilgamesh is blaming Ishtar for. A peculiarly close resemblance is that Aphrodite has a mother in this scene, Dione, who apparently dwells on Olympus as Zeus's wife; Hera is out of the picture for the moment. Olympian Dione makes her appearance solely in this scene, nowhere else.[78] Undoubtedly even in antiquity the contrast here to the account of Aphrodite's birth from the sea in Hesiod, after the castration of Uranus, was disconcerting. It is true that Dione, together with Zeus, is attested in the cult of Dodona; and a goddess Diwija appears at Mycenaean Pylos. At any rate, the mother of Aphrodite is given a crystal-clear Greek name here: "Dione" is just the feminine form of Zeus. This is unique in the Homeric family of gods, where couples have complicated individual names. But this detail has its exact counterpart in the Akkadian text: Antu the mother of Ishtar is the feminine form of Anu, Heaven, with the common feminine suffix. This divine couple, Mr. and Mrs. Heaven, is firmly established in the worship and mythology of Mesopotamia. Homer proves to be dependent on *Gilgamesh* even at the linguistic level, introducing Dione as a calque on Antu in the Olympic family just for one impressive scene among the gods; after this Dione disappears and Hera is again present. The Greek-Akkadian connection is no less impressive than in the case of Tethys-Tawtu, here at the level of narrative structure and divine characters instead of cosmic agents.

Of course there are differences too. Ishtar's meeting with Gilgamesh is firmly anchored in the structure of the *Gilgamesh* epic; it constitutes the narrative link from the Humbaba theme to the next heroic deed, the struggle with the bull of heaven. It is Ishtar, in her wrath, who brings down the bull of heaven to make his attack. This gives Gilgamesh and Enkidu the opportunity of killing the bull and thus establishing sacrifice. A ritual background is clear, even in details. Gilgamesh's rejection of Ishtar corresponds to the hunters' taboo: sexual acts drive the animals away, as Enkidu has experienced;[79] sexual restraint is supposed to attract them. The denial of love causes the bull to appear. The transfor-

mations of Ishtar's lovers as reported in Gilgamesh's catalogue
have their special meaning and context too. Some are myths
about the process of civilization: in this way the horse was domes-
ticated.[80] What has remained in Homer is the narrative thread of
a genre scene, depicted with gusto all the more because it is, on
the whole, without function. It has its own charm within the
framework of the *Iliad,* but does not carry comparable weight
either in the course of the narrative or in relation to a ritual
background. The manner in which Akkadian demons have been
turned into fantastic monsters, more amusing than frightening—
Lamashtu transformed into the Gorgon[81]—has its counterpart on
the level of epic poetry about the gods.

The influence of *Gilgamesh* may also be detected in a scene
from the *Odyssey.* In it Homer describes a form of prayer that
puzzled historians of religion. When Penelope learns about the
risky journey undertaken by Telemachus and about the suitors'
plot to kill him, she first bursts into tears and complaints. Then,
calming down, she washes and dresses in clean clothes and goes
up to the upper story of the house, together with her maids, taking barley corn in a basket. She prays to Athena for safe return of
Telemachus, and ends with an inarticulate shriek *(ololyge).* Both
the basket with barley and the cry have their proper place in
blood sacrifice, but their use in this scene is strange and unparal-
leled elsewhere. So scholars spoke either of an "abbreviation of
sacrifice" or of an otherwise unknown ritual of vegetarian offering, or even of an invention of the poet, if not incompetence
of the redactor. But look at *Gilgamesh.* When Gilgamesh and
Enkidu leave the city to fight Humbaba, the hero's mother, Nin-
sun, offers a ceremonial prayer. She cleans herself in water, she
puts on a fine garment. "She went up the stairs, she climbed on
to the roof, to Shamash (the Sun god) she set up incense, she
brought the offering and raised her hands before Shamash"; in
this form she prays, full of distress and sorrow, for the safe return

of her son.[82] The situation, mother praying for an adventurous son, is not a special one. Yet in its details the scene from the *Odyssey* comes close to being a translation of *Gilgamesh;* in fact it is closer to the *Gilgamesh* text than to the comparable scene in the *Iliad,* when Achilles is praying for a safe return of Patroclus, with a ceremonial libation of wine.[83] What appears odd in the ritual of the *Odyssey* is quite at home in *Gilgamesh:* burning incense on the roof is a well known Semitic practice, all the more when one turns to the Sun god. In Greece, prayer in the women's upper story is unheard of.[84] It seems the poet knew that burning incense was out of place in the world of Greek heroes; so he took the female part of normal sacrifice as a substitute, barley basket and *ololyge.* This use of religious ritual as an effective motif precisely in this situation has its antecedent in the oriental tradition.

One further detail from the *Odyssey:* when Philoitios the herdsman beholds Odysseus the beggar—his master in disguise—he bursts into a strange complaint: "Father Zeus, no god is more destructive than you are: you have no compassion for men, after you have engendered them yourself."[85] How can Philoitios claim that Zeus has engendered men himself? Greek myth is not explicit about this. Commentaries remain vague. By the way, this may be the earliest Greek expression of the antithesis of "generation" and "destruction" which was to dominate natural philosophy. It leads back to Eastern reflections about creation in general. In Akkadian as in Hebrew we find the maxim that creation by a god entails an obligation of this god toward his creature. "What you have created, do not destroy" is a common form of prayer. The gods themselves are heard to ask, "Why should we destroy what we have created?"[86] To reproach the god who destroys what he has himself created thus turns out to be an oriental motif—with the modification that the Greek poet would think of a god who engenders rather than creates.

Another, more distanced reflection of *Atrahasis* may be found in the *Iliad*. One of the most dramatic episodes right at the beginning of the Babylonian poem is the strike of the lower gods against Enlil, their boss. They are tired of doing all the toilsome work with canals and dikes; so they burn their implements and gather in front of the "house"—the temple—of Enlil at night. Not surprisingly, Enlil becomes quite nervous, and he quickly sends a messenger to Anu in heaven and another to Enki in the depths of the waters; both instantly come to give their advice; the outcome will be the creation of human robots.[87] In the first book of the *Iliad*, Thetis tells a story which does not otherwise appear anywhere else, about "how the other gods of Olympus wanted to fetter Zeus"; no motive is given for such a revolution in the palace. But in this situation Thetis acted as a messenger on her own account; she made the powerful Briareus-Aegaeon come up from the depths of the sea. He sat down at Zeus's side and with his ferocious aspect scared the other gods away.[88] The correspondence with *Atrahasis* is not very close; stories of quarrels among the gods are not uncommon. Yet a collective insurrection against the ruling god of heaven and the help that came from deep waters is somewhat more specific. And since connections between Eastern and Greek epics are established anyway, we are inclined to take into consideration the Eastern model even in this case. Once more we find that what had been an integral element of the main story in *Atrahasis* has been demoted to a passing incident, an unconnected improvisation without precedent or consequence. It is characteristic that it should appear in a tale told by a god.

Some threads lead from cunning Atrahasis to the Prometheus myth too.[89] But these are both complex and less specific when set against the background of the common trickster figure and trickster mythology which extends far beyond the Near Eastern-Greece axis.

Affinities and similarities between oriental epic and Homeric poetry can no longer be ignored in interpreting Homer. This means that certain limits must be set to deriving Homer in his totality either from purely Indoeuropean stock or from Mycenaean prehistory. Homeric epic is a many-sided phenomenon. The Eastern influence is most marked in scenes of the divine pantheon, where characters, plots, and basic ideas seem to be borrowed. It would be wrong to overemphasize similarities or to overlook the marked differences. But never forget that we are dealing with civilizations which were close to each other in time and space and which had continuous demonstrable contact. To insist on completely separate developments and purely coincidental parallels is to beg the question.

Chronology has always been a problem within the Homeric genre. It has proved difficult to arrive at objective criteria to separate later and secondary elements from the original bedrock. As regards the most striking oriental connections, whether in the Deception of Zeus or in the *Cypria,* the clues do not point to very great age. Tales of heroic combat, on the other hand, definitely go back to the Bronze Age, with Ramses' account of his chariot fight in the battle of Qadesh. Of course Bronze Age heritage could subsequently be revitalized by more recent input. Just one example: besides the old and normal Greek loan word for "lion," *leon,* possibly of Egyptian origin, another word was adopted in some Homeric similes, *lis,* and this clearly has a Semitic-Palestinian pedigree.[90] Maybe this points to the orientalizing epoch of the eighth and seventh centuries, in contrast to an older Bronze Age layer.

The formation of the first Greek library—thus we might imagine the *Iliad* in its earliest written form, written down on 24 (?) leather scrolls—may be practically contemporary with the great enterprise of Assurbanipal (668–627), his library at Nineveh.[91] Even this may not be pure coincidence; remember the King's Road opened by the initiative of Gyges. The Semitic East still held the cultural lead at that date; the breakdown of the Assyrian empire made room for new developments.

One last observation. Both passages of Akkadian classics which resonate so notably in the Deception of Zeus, Apsu and Tiamat mingling their waters, and the three gods throwing lots about the partition of the universe, come from the very beginnings of the respective texts, *Enuma Elish* and *Atrahasis,* mythological texts which were particularly well known and frequently used; these texts were even used in school curricula.[92] For young students the emphasis naturally is on the opening section. Many will recall *arma virumque cano* from their schooldays, and little more of Vergil, or also the first line of the *Odyssey.* Thus we may imagine a Greek, seeking education, to be acquainted with precisely these sections of classical Eastern literature, either directly or indirectly via Aramaic versions, even if he did not make very much progress in his curriculum. In any case, school tradition on an elementary level is inherent in the transmission of the alphabet to Greece. Indeed, the various channels of transmission considered here—iconography, tales, rituals, curiosity, or even school—are in no way mutually exclusive. They may have overlapped and reinforced one another in many different ways. Be that as it may, the conclusion is that Homer's *Iliad* bears the mark, at least at some probably late stage, of the orientalizing impact.[93] Classical scholars should no longer ignore the nearest parallels and partial antecedents of the oldest Greek poetry.

3

Oriental Wisdom Literature and Cosmogony

A very special form of thought and literature made its appearance in Greece by the second half of the sixth century. In retrospect we call it the beginnings of natural philosophy, or Presocratic philosophy. Its pursuits include an intensified interest in and knowledge of the realm of science, notably astronomy, and in mathematics, which moved from practice to theory, from counting to demonstration. The process has often been described, and attempts at causal explanation are not lacking. But what is left from the earliest Greek texts of this period is so fragmentary that we can hardly hope for a comprehensive and distinct view.

At any rate, what is seldom fully acknowledged is that this new intellectual enterprise came to the fore with the establishment of the Achaemenid empire. The fame of Thales is linked to a solar eclipse—probably in 586 B.C.—in the midst of conflict between Lydians, Iranian Medes, and Babylonians, after the annihilation of Assyrian Nineveh. Anaximander is said to have published his book in 547 B.C., the very year in which Cyrus conquered Sardis, took over the Lydian kingdom, and thus founded the Persian empire, an empire that included the Greeks of Asia Minor from the start. Xenophanes of Colophon left Ionia "when the Mede arrived" (B 22). Heraclitus stayed at Ephesus and maintained relations with the Artemision, the sanctuary of international fame which emphatically accepted Persian rule by assigning a Persian title to its main priest: Megabyxos.[1] Scylax of Caryanda in Caria, the first Greek writer on geography, traveled to India in the service of King Darius (Herodotus 4.44). If books with a wider scope on the universe and its origin came to be written just in this epoch, they did not thrive in a vacuum. They drew from older contexts beyond provincial borders, mainly two currents of thought and literature which were widespread: pronouncements of wisdom and cosmogonic mythology.

The hypothesis or suspicion that Greek philosophy was not an original invention of the Greeks but copied from more ancient Eastern prototypes is not a modern one. It goes right back to Aristotle's book *On Philosophy (Peri philosophias)* and to Aristotle's pupils who discussed *barbaros philosophia*. They took account, of course, of Egyptians, Chaldaeans, Iranian magi including Zoroaster, Indian gurus, and Jews.[2] The last head of the Neoplatonic Academy in Athens, Damascius, in his book on *First Principles,* offers interpretations of the cosmogonies of the Babylonians, the magi, and the Phoenicians, quoting from a book by Eudemus, Aristotle's well-known pupil. It contained, among other information, a close paraphrase of the first lines of the Babylonian *Enuma Elish*.[3] By then the thesis about *barbaros philosophia* had long been appropriated by Jews and Christians for their own purposes. Noting that Moses had lived many centuries before Plato, they argued that Plato had taken all essentials of his philosophy—his theology most of all—from Israel.[4] What is Plato if not a Moses speaking Attic, Numenius asked.[5] In these ancient discussions the global direction was quite unimportant: no trace of an East-West or a North-South conflict.

The scholarly history of philosophy as developed in the nineteenth century resumed the discussion, with changed results. Most significant in the field was, after Hegel, the view of Eduard

Zeller. In the introduction to his magnificent work *Die Philosophie der Griechen in ihrer geschichtlichen Entwicklung,* first published in 1856, Zeller presented a critical review of earlier works that suggested Chinese, Indian, and other precursors of Greek philosophy, and he rejected them all.[6] Zeller's position and arguments predominated down to the middle of the twentieth century.

As a consequence of Zeller's idea that Greek philosophy is self-generated, pure Greek in origin, the scholarly world nearly overlooked a radical development that occurred after his treatise had been published: the emergence of original texts of Eastern literatures, first Egyptian and Mesopotamian, then Hittite and Ugaritic. Up to this point, not much from pre-Greek antiquity had been known other than the Hebrew Bible, and philologists easily showed that this had not been accessible to Greeks before the Hellenistic period. The Iranian *Avesta* had been edited and translated by 1771,[7] but this remained a marginal curiosity. Yet these ancient Near Eastern texts were to throw new light on the old question. It turned out that neither Hebrew nor Greek, neither Moses nor Homer, marked the beginning of literature, but rather pyramid texts and Sumerian myths. The problem of the context in which Greek philosophy evolved from the sixth to the fourth century B.C. was given new horizons. As I already mentioned,[8] it was an outsider, William Gladstone, who in 1890 referred to a parallel of cosmogonic myth in *Enuma Elish* and in the *Iliad.* Yet it was not until 1941 that Francis Macdonald Cornford, in a Cambridge lecture, presented a careful comparison between Hesiod and *Enuma Elish;* this was published in 1950.[9] By then the newly found Hittite texts also helped to break the barrier between the Greek and Semitic worlds. In the wake of Hittite, Ugaritic too was easily accepted. At this time Uvo Hölscher outlined the new perspectives in his fascinating paper "Anaximandros und der Anfang der Philosophie"; Hans Schwabl followed suit; Martin West's commentaries on Hesiod are full of pertinent information and reflection; and a sober and informative book by Peter Walcot appeared in 1966.[10]

The opening of new horizons coincided with a change in the concept of philosophy. The moderns lost interest in rational ontology in the wake of Aristotle and scholasticism; Aristotle and even Plato's realm of ideas seemed less and less attractive. This meant fresh and keen interest in the Presocratics, especially in Heraclitus and Parmenides, from Karl Reinhardt via Martin Heidegger to Hans Georg Gadamer;[11] it went together with an intense interest in myth. Many thinkers were inclined to perceive some original synthesis or at any rate some continuous transition from myth to philosophy. Take the title of Olof Gigon's book of 1945: *Der Ursprung der griechischen Philosophie von Hesiod bis Parmenides,*[12] which includes Hesiod in the origin of Greek philosophy and postulates a culmination in Parmenides. Just in those years, however, the Hittite texts about Kumarbi were published, which drew Hesiod into the oriental maelstrom[13]—Olof Gigon did not like this, but it could not be undone.

After some decades of relative quiet, interest in ancient cross-cultural penetration has been rising again—not without uneasiness, and not only under the impact of Martin Bernal's *Black Athena.*[14] Do we really owe some decisive development to the Greeks, and in what sense? Philosophy and science seem to be at the center of answers in the affirmative; but corroboration cannot be achieved without full view of the oriental background and alternatives.

In the midst of uncertainties and changing paradigms, two incontrovertible facts remain. First, philosophy up to now has been defined by the direct tradition of, and the direct connection with, Greek texts which have been studied for almost 2400 years; second, the first high cultures practicing literacy did not emerge in Europe, but in the fertile crescent from Iraq through Syria and

Palestine to Egypt, with extensions to Iran and to Anatolia. These people were not necessarily less sophisticated than the Greeks.

As to the first statement, there is no question about the continuity of philosophy, under this name. It is based on the works of Plato and Aristotle which, together with subsequent books, were studied throughout antiquity. They reached the Romans, were transmitted to Persians and Arabs in translation, and via those works became known in medieval Europe, later to be followed by the Greek originals. These texts are still to be found in every philosophical library, in diverse translations and editions. Alfred North Whitehead remarked that philosophy was nothing but "some comments on Plato."[15] Plato, in turn, was not an absolutely new beginning; he read and criticized Heraclitus, Parmenides, Anaxagoras, Empedocles, Protagoras, and other sophists; we speak of the Presocratics now, but should rather say Preplatonics. Aristotle, his pupil, read and criticized Plato and all the other writers, including the atomists Leucippus and Democritus. Since then philosophy has been a critical dialogue with these fundamental texts; nobody has been able to reinvent philosophy because it was always there. Even if philosophy is anything but certain about its own identity, the very question "what is philosophy" is inseparably bound to the Greek foundation.

Indeed, there is no comparable tradition of books, texts, and translations which goes back beyond Parmenides, Heraclitus, and Anaximander. As far as we know, there are no direct translations at all in Greek literature before Hellenistic times—whereas Latin literature began with translations from the Greek. No doubt writing as such, together with the book scroll and the writing tablet, came from Syria to Greece in the eighth century. But we cannot point to any oriental work which a Greek person of the eighth or seventh century has demonstrably read or seen. The first Greek books we can enumerate were poetry, Hesiod, Homer, perhaps oracles;[16] and poetry is bound to a single mother tongue more than other genres. Only when Greek civilization had reached its special level and was being accepted as a model in the whole of the Mediterranean world—that is, only in the second half of the sixth century—did those works appear which we take to be the beginnings of Greek philosophy, by Anaximander and Heraclitus and other Presocratics.

Yet literature, highly developed literature which can be studied in detail, did exist in the East. And it is easy to see that what we call early Greek philosophy is indebted to earlier traditions in a twofold way: the elaboration of cosmogonic myth, or stories of creation, as we may also call them, and the composition of wisdom literature. Both types appear, not by coincidence, in Hesiod's two works, *Theogony* (including the *Catalogues*) and *Works and Days.* These two works seem to come close to the date when Greeks first borrowed the alphabet. In addition, a growing store of geographical, astronomical, and mathematical knowledge seems to accumulate in Greek culture in the following centuries, parallel to what we can call Babylonian science.

Before going into details, the social context or medium of philosophizing should be considered, including the problem of orality versus literacy. For 2400 years philosophy has existed in the form of the philosophical book. Plato criticized literacy, but was himself the first abundantly productive and successful prose writer. All the same, philosophical books always originated and came to life in circles of discussion, in schools of philosophy. Plato set the example with his own Academy, and similar institutions existed with varied success down to the end of antiquity and were resuscitated in the universities and academies of Europe.

We are much less well informed about the situation before Plato. We are told that Anaximander's book was the first work in prose ever published[17]—in what context? We are told that Heraclitus dedicated his book in the temple of Artemis at Ephesus[18]— to be read, or to be preserved in seclusion, unavailable? Practical handbooks of astronomy and geography which began to circulate in the sixth century were obviously useful. A *Nautike Astrologia* was attributed to Thales;[19] Scylax of Caryanda wrote a *periegesis*;[20] Hecataeus wrote on geography and presented a map of the earth as it had been designed first by Anaximander.[21] In addition, genealogical handbooks were written in prose, by Hecataeus of Miletus, by Acusilaus of Argos, and by Pherecydes of Athens.[22] Both the astronomical-geographical and the genealogical handbooks are, as it were, modernizations of Hesiod's *Theogony* and *Works and Days,* ending in astronomy. Acusilaus had theogony precede his genealogy. From about the same time, say 500 B.C., we know of another book that begins with the creation of the world and continues with the development of the tribes which constitute the people: *Bereshit,* the book of Genesis in its final redaction, may belong to this very period.

So much for books; it is difficult to find evidence for philosophical schools before Plato, even if later doxography has constructed "successions." We are vaguely informed about the "sect" of the Pythagoreans[23] and about personal relations between Parmenides and Zeno: Parmenides adopted Zeno, we are told.[24] This indicates quite an old and ubiquitous model of the tradition of knowledge, especially secret knowledge, as being passed on within a "family," whether among craftsmen, seers, magicians, doctors, or poets. "The knowing one shall instruct the knowing one," as a cuneiform formula reads.[25] Frequently myths are put to use in rituals for healing the sick:[26] mythology too is transmitted in such a way. The doctors of Cos were all Asclepiads. "Heracliteans" are mentioned in the fifth century; it is not known for certain whether they just accidentally read and imitated the book of Heraclitus or had some organization and connection with one another.

The Eastern world, however, sustained another kind of quite different institutions for the tradition of knowledge: the temples, which existed as economically independent and self-supporting units and which fed a community of priests; to these usually was attached a school of writing, "the house of tablets." Because the complicated old systems of writing, which continued to be in full use throughout the first millennium B.C., necessitated professional training that lasted for years, the house of tablets would constitute the credentials for the self-consciousness of "the knowing ones," the experts. A wise man is a "lord of tablets." In Egypt the very idea of immortality originates in the writing of the scribes.[27] Note that any school of writing needs convenient texts for exercise; and what makes the contents of a primer? Sayings and simple narratives—that is, wisdom literature and mythology. So this is one of the "social places" for the literature we are interested in. Mythology was also used in hymns and other ritual texts to celebrate various gods; *Enuma Elish* belongs to the New Year festival of Babylon—with other versions for other places. Wisdom literature also tended to appeal to kings and sought to profit from their authority, be it Solomon or another monarch.

The Greeks lacked this structure: they had neither economically independent temples supporting communities of priests nor associated houses of tablets; and kings too were soon shunted aside. Alphabetic writing is so easy to learn and to practice that no class distinction could emerge from elementary school; it was left to the sophists to invent higher education as a new form of class distinction. Yet deficit was turned into progress: in Greece cultural knowledge became separated from dominating institutions and hierarchies, from the house of tablets, from temples, and from kingship; it became movable, and the property of individuals. Of course, the western Semites from Tarsus through Tyre to Jerusalem could have taken advantage of the same opportunity, for they used a nearly identical variety of alphabetic writing; but they were harassed and impeded by the destructive invasions of Assyrians and Babylonians. The Greeks, living further west, were close to these events but remained nearly unaffected. The Jews, in the midst of troubles, preserved their own identity through the constraining decision to make Scripture their highest authority, instead of using it as the decisive tool of spiritual freedom.

Let us take a look at wisdom literature first. This is fully developed in Egyptian, Sumerian, Akkadian, and Hurrian traditions,[28] and not least in the Hebrew Bible. See the sayings of Solomon, the Book of Proverbs, in fact a collection of collections. Among Greek texts, parts of Hesiod are prominent examples, then Phocylides and Theognis, and the tradition of the Seven Sages, which is set in the period around 600 B.C. While this teaching was still in part oral, written texts to continue the tradition emerge within the Hippocratean Corpus—the Aphorisms—with Democritus, Isocrates, and others, down to a much more recent and highly original collection such as the *logia* of Jesus.[29]

Wisdom literature brings in various sayings to constitute general rules, in the form of imperatives, statements, or even short stories; thus animal and plant fables too belong to the genre.[30] Highly developed literary forms, such as dialogues, emerge in Egypt, in Mesopotamia, and in the Book of Job. Sometimes a certain situation is evoked, with kings entering the scene: the Egyptian *The Instruction of King Amenemhet I for his son Sesostris I*,[31] and the Sumerian *The Instructions of Shuruppak to his son Ziusudra*—Ziusudra who was to survive the flood. In the Hebrew Bible we find the *Proverbs of Solomon son of David, king of Israel,* and also *Sayings of Lemuel king of Massa, which his mother taught him* (Proverbs 31). Compare the *Admonitions of Hesiod to his brother Perses,* as *Works and Days* has been titled by moderns, or *Counsels of Chiron to Achilles (Chironos Hypothekai)*.[32] A more thrilling story is introduced in the Aramaic text of Achiquar, which became known also to the Greeks.[33] Achiquar is slandered by his nephew, whereupon the king takes him to jail; when his innocence has been proved and Achiquar is released, he gets a chance to transmit his wisdom to the bad nephew by flogging: one blow for each counsel.

Wisdom sayings are seldom arranged in any order or system. If there is causal reasoning, it goes just one step forward; this is not philosophical ethics. Collections may include sophisticated literary devices such as acrostics,[34] elaborate antitheses and striking metaphors, and also riddles. "A capable wife is her husband's crown; one who disgraces him is like rot in his bones" (Proverbs 12.4). Hesiod makes the same statement without metaphor: "Nothing better than a wife a man has seized as his booty, a good one—but nothing is more horrible than a bad one" (*Works and Days* 702 f.).

Wisdom literature is an intellectual accomplishment that goes beyond trivialities. The texts show a deliberate working with language, with analogies and antithesis; the whole enterprise is based on the hypothesis, which is anything but obvious, that it is helpful to have wisdom, that it pays to learn from wise men—an optimism of *logos,* one might say. The postulate of generalization assumes that the wise man's counsel is valid always and everywhere, beyond the moment—even if the counsel may be to guard the moment *(kairos).*

At times the optimism of *logos* has its limits; it may touch the frontiers of cynicism. Sometimes unabashed egotism is promoted, such as in the warning not to take up pledges; Solomon and the Sages agree fully on this point.[35] "Most people are bad"; this too is a saying of the Sages.[36] And is it really true that "wisdom is more valuable than gold" (Proverbs 23.14)? Does piety pay? The text of Job probes the question with painful insistence. The so-called Babylonian theodicy reads: "Those who neglect the gods go the way of prosperity, while those who pray to the goddess are impoverished and dispossessed."[37]

Nonetheless *logos* optimism is prone to entail a form of moral-

ity that relies on reason as against the emotions, extolling ratio-
nality, moderation, self-control, justice, and piety, and warning
against hot temper, drunkenness, and sexual indulgence. "Avarice
is a grievous and incurable illness," the Egyptians say; "better one
bread with a happy heart than riches with trouble"[38]; and "moderation is best," the Seven Sages preach.[39] Stability is desirable,
even if it is difficult to attain. A certain verse of Homer, Odysseus' warning to the suitor Amphinomus, made a lasting impres-
sion on Greek readers: "Such is the insight *(nous)* of men on earth
as is the day which Zeus, the father of men and gods, brings on,"
meaning that it is unreliable and changeable from brightness to
gloom. An Akkadian text makes a similar comment on man's
condition: "Their insight changes like day and night: when starv-
ing they become like corpses, when replete they vie with their
gods."[40] A proverb from the world of animals rose to prominence
when the Cologne papyrus of Archilochus became known: "Being hasty, the bitch gives birth to blind puppies"; the same proverb appears in a text from Mari about 1000 years before Archilochus.[41]

Ethics of moderation come to dominate the outlines of cosmology. The two lines of thought before philosophy which we
are following, wisdom and cosmogony, come in touch. "In wisdom the Lord founded the earth, and by understanding he set the
heavens in their place" (Proverbs 3.19). Wisdom itself proclaims:
"When he set the heavens in their place I was there, when he gir-
dled the ocean with the horizon, when he fixed the canopy of
clouds overhead . . . when he prescribed its limits to the sea . . .
then I was at his side each day" (Proverbs 8.27–30). Egyptians
have Ma'at, Order, marching at the side of the Sun god;[42] Babylonians have Misharu, Just Order, in the same place and function. "Helios will not transgress his boundaries," Heraclitus
wrote, "or else the Erinyes, the helpers of Justice, will find him
out."[43] Anaximander declares that the "things that exist," *ta eonta,*

"pay penalty and retribution to each other for their injustice according to the assessment of Time."[44] He was probably thinking
of the order of day and year, which indeed cover shortage by ex-
cess and vice versa. Cosmic order is the paradigm of justice,
whether it is said that Maat or Misharu accompany the Sun, or
that the Erinyes watch out for any transgression. In the words of
Parmenides, justice holds the alternating keys for day and night.[45]
"This world order . . . it always was, and is, and shall be: an ever-
living fire, kindling in measures and going out in measures"—this
is Heraclitus,[46] whose "measures" mark out a new dimension of
thinking while still proceeding from the same traditional basis of
justice, measure for measure alternating in time, the paradigm of
the cosmic order.

Even the special vigor of Heraclitus' wisdom can be seen more
clearly against the background of traditional wisdom literature.
The beginning of Solomon's proverbs—with slight abbreviation—reads: "Proverbs of Solomon son of David . . . by which
. . . the simple will be endowed with shrewdness, and . . . if the
wise man listens, he will increase his learning."[47] Contrast the beginning of Heraclitus' book: "*Logos* of Heraclitus, son of Bloson:
Of this *logos*, which is always, men prove to be uncomprehending, both before they have heard it and once they have heard it
for the first time; for although all things come to pass in accor-
dance with this *logos*, men behave as if they were ignorant of it."[48]
This sounds like a scornful parody of the normal and naive prem-
ise of wisdom, which is to teach those who don't know and to im-
prove those who do know. No, says Heraclitus, men prove to be
uncomprehending, even if things that come to pass are burning
at their fingertips. This definitely goes beyond the statement that
wisdom was there when limits were prescribed to the sea. But it
presupposes the traditional approach of wisdom.

We have already entered the field of cosmogony and found
continuities as well as unforeseeable "fulgurations," sudden
changes within an uninterrupted evolution.

As to the beginning of the world, many tales propose numerous variants. The model, as it were, is set by the Babylonian text *Enuma Elish,* the epic of creation recited at the Babylonian New Year Festival.[49] Egypt has no one representative text but rather several groups of texts, some fully developed and others of allusive character, usually reflecting the position of one particular sanctuary: the cosmogony of Heliopolis, of Memphis, of Hermopolis.[50] Hittite presents the Kumarbi text, which is especially close to Hesiod.[51] And let us not forget the beginning of the Bible, which has cosmogony or rather creation in two different tales.[52]

Cosmogony has always been highly speculative. The form of the narrative is naive; it is a typical just-so story—a term of scorn for anthropologists.[53] "In the beginning there was . . . then came . . . and then . . ."—just so. First the world was not there, then Heaven and Earth appeared, and gods, and men, and their relation was set right, just so. The so-called first philosophers among the Greeks do not disdain this form of account: "Together were all the things," Anaxagoras started, "and as they were together nothing was explicit, because fog and brilliant haze held down everything"[54]—how close this is to "and the earth was without form and void, with darkness over the face of the abyss" (Genesis 1.2). Yet the very concept of beginning is a speculative achievement— one beginning from which everything is about to rise. Note that archaic language usually does not have a word for "world"; it enumerates the basic constituents, above all heaven and earth: "In the beginning, the Lord created heaven and earth"; but there should have been a unity before duality.

Further steps of speculation are reversal and antithesis. If you start to tell the tale about the beginning of everything, you must first delete everything from your view, the whole world of ours, people and animals, houses and trees, mountains and sea, heaven and earth. Thus the typical start of cosmogonic myth is performed by subtraction: there is a great and resounding "Not Yet."

Enuma Elish starts: "When above skies were not named, nor earth below pronounced by name . . . [when nobody] had formed pastures nor discovered reed beds, when no gods were manifest, nor names pronounced, nor destinies decreed."[55] An Egyptian pyramid text says: "When heaven had not yet been constructed, when earth had not yet come into being, when nothing yet had been constructed"[56]—what was there? "Darkness hovering upon the face of the deep," the Bible tells us;[57] a yawning gap, *chaos,* Hesiod has it;[58] Night, in the theogony of Orpheus;[59] the Infinite, Anaximander is said to have written. "Together were all the things," we read in Anaxagoras.[60] But the most frequent account says that in the beginning there was Water. This is not limited to the ancient Mediterranean world, it is also reported from America.[61] Water is the beginning, Thales is reported to have said;[62] but long before him the Egyptians had developed water cosmogonies in several variants;[63] and *Enuma Elish* too has ground water and salt water mingling, namely Apsu the begetter and Tiamat who bore them all, the first parents of everything. This recurs in the *Iliad* with Oceanus and Tethys, "begetting everything."[64]

The whole must break up. Differentiation must come out of the single beginning. Every cosmogonic tale is bound to proceed on these lines. The most grandiose idea is that heaven was lifted from earth at the second state of creation, that the world qua "heaven and earth" came into being by separation. Even this idea is not a specialty of the ancient Mediterranean world; it has been found in Africa, Polynesia, and Japan.[65] Hittites, Hesiod, and Orpheus offer the violent myth of a castration of Heaven, of cutting apart the primeval couple.[66] Egyptians have a more peaceful development, as Shu, "Air," just lifts Nut the goddess of heaven from the earth, Geb. Heaven is female in this case.[67] According to Anaximander a sphere of fire grew around the center, which apparently was a form of slime; the sphere then burst into pieces which formed into wheels, carrying openings of flames around the earth.[68] This still results in the separation of heaven and earth.

For the further development, there are two narrative options, two models: one might be called biomorphic, the other techno-morphic. The biomorphic model introduces couples of different sex; it has insemination and birth. The technomorphic model presents a creator in the function of a superb craftsman. The biomorphic model gives rise to successive generations of gods, with chances for a battle between Old and New. The succession myth is found in *Enuma Elish,* in the Hittite and Phoenician versions, and in Hesiod and Orpheus.[69] It is tempting to call the biomorphic model the Greek one, the technomorphic model the biblical one. Hesiod has fully opted for the biomorphic version, whereas Genesis is the definite book of creation: "And god made." He carved Eve from a rib, and he even fabricated the first garments.[70] The textual evidence is more complicated though. The craftsman's job is at times sublimated when he just gives commands, "and so it was"; this applies to Genesis, to Egyptian Ptah, and also to a test Marduk undergoes in *Enuma Elish.*[71] Even more sublime is a creator who works by thinking, as Xenophanes, Orpheus, and Parmenides describe him, an idea also mentioned in Egyptian texts.[72] Yet we also find important combinations of both models, such as in *Enuma Elish* and in the Orphic cosmogony, known from the Derveni papyrus: they introduce some generations of gods first, but then concentrate on one god who is planning his creation.[73] Creation in such a case is in fact more rational; it provides the opportunity for describing objects in detail. But it cannot start from zero, since the creator must already be there. In *Enuma Elish,* when Marduk has slain Tiamat, the primeval mother, the monster of the sea,

> the Lord rested and inspected her corpse, he divided the monstrous shape and created marvels. He sliced her in half like a fish for drying, half of her he put up to roof the sky [separating heaven and earth] as for the stars, he set up constellations . . . he made the crescent of the moon appear, en-

trusted night to it . . . [addressing the moon] Go forth every
month without fail in a corona, at the beginning of the
month, to glow over the land; you shine with horns to mark
out six days; on the seventh day the crown is half. The fif-
teenth day shall always be the mid-point, the half of each
month. When Shamash [sun] looks at you from the horizon, gradually shed your visibility and begin to wane.[74]

This astronomical job description is perhaps not exciting, but
quite correct. The Hebrew Bible is much more cursory. Elohim
said: "Let there be lights in the vault of heaven to separate day
from night . . . And God made the two great lights, the greater to
govern the day and the lesser to govern the night, and with them
he made the stars."[75] Least precise is Hesiod: "Theia gave birth to
great Helios (Sun) and resplendent Selene (Moon), and also to
Eos (Dawn) who shines for all on earth, overcome in love by
Hyperion; and Eos, mated to Astraios, gave birth to the Morning
Star, and to the brilliant Stars."[76] Nobody would say Hesiod is
more rational than the oriental texts. He gives names to the concepts of "divine" (Theia), and "walking above" (Hyperion). But it
is unsystematic to arrange Dawn with the constellations; it is just
tautology to make Astraios father of the stars; and it is arbitrary
to separate the Morning Star from the other stars because it is
somehow born in dawn.

Heraclitus explicitly rejects the concept of creator of the world:
"This world order . . . no one of gods or men has made" (B 30).
He seems to develop the biomorphic model into a phytomorphic
one, the principle of growing according to inner laws, as the
plants do; the Greek word for such growing is *physis,* which later
was translated into Latin as *natura.* It is considered the very
catchword of Greek philosophy of nature, though the concept
reached its full development only about two generations after
Heraclitus. Heraclitus' much quoted saying that "Nature loves to

be concealed" takes its start from a limited yet precise observation: if you dig up the earth to see the germ growing, you will destroy the plant.[77] Heraclitus thus rejects cosmic craftsmanship. But hardly any of his successors can do without the concept of creator. Thus Parmenides introduces a female *daimon* who governs everything and creates divine powers such as Eros by her planning;[78] Anaxagoras assigns a similar function to Nous, Mind, the leading power for all differentiation; Empedocles has Love, also called the goddess Aphrodite, constructing living organisms in her workshop. Democritus was the only one who (in criticizing Anaxagoras) tried to exclude Mind from the shaping of macrocosm and microcosm; he proposed what we now call self-organization.[79] The reaction came with Plato and Aristotle; Plato's *Timaeus* finally established the term "creator," *demiourgos,* in Greek philosophy.

So far there is no reason to separate the mythical cosmogonies of the Greeks—Homer, Hesiod, or Orpheus—from their Eastern counterparts. They evidently belong to the same family, and it is no less evident that the Presocratics still follow in their steps.

Let us just briefly recall that in some more rational fields the Greeks' dependence upon Mesopotamia is uncommonly clear: mathematics and astronomy. The so-called Pythagorean theorem is routinely applied in cuneiform texts about 1000 years before Pythagoras. Our names for the planets Mercury, Venus, Mars, and Jupiter are indirect translations from the Akkadian designations, via the Greek names which directly rendered Nabu, Ishtar, Nergal, and Marduk.[80] The division of the circle into 360 degrees, with subsections of 60 minutes and 60 seconds, is the most direct Babylonian legacy with which schoolchildren still struggle today; in Greece it may have been adopted only after Alexander.[81]

The connections between Eastern and Greek speculation are not limited to one narrow interlude, say around 700 B.C., from Hittite Cilicia and Phoenician Syria to Hesiod. To the contrary,

continuous contacts took place, as can be seen when we compare
the theogonies of the *Iliad,* of Hesiod, and of Orpheus, each of
which has special points of contact with Akkadian, Hittite, and
Phoenician texts. The theogony of Orpheus has the god swallowing a phallus, as does Kumarbi; this is not in Hesiod.[82] The cosmic detail ascribed to Thales that earth is built on water like a
ship has parallels neither in Homer nor in Hesiod, but it comes
up in the Bible and in Akkadian myth. In the sixth century Iranian elements begin to play a role. The sequence of stars, moon,
and sun in Anaximander's "wheels," in flagrant contrast to our
scientific knowledge, agrees with the Iranian ascent to heaven.[83]
Zarathustra's religion taught that the human soul, after death,
rises to a realm of light in heaven, and variants of such an idea
show up in the thinking of the Presocratics.[84] In other words, a
large zone of East-West contacts and interactions can be taken for
granted.

Certainly we should keep in mind that Eastern cultures do not
represent only the pre-rational, the mythical stage, leaving it to
the Greeks to march the whole way from *mythos* to *logos.* The dependence of the Greeks is most evident in certain areas of astronomy. In this field Babylonians developed absolutely rational
methods of computing,[85] whereas in their cosmogony myth continued to loom large, as it did for the Greeks. Even in cosmology
the oriental scholars, in Assyria, for example, were already on the
road from myth to speculation. Let us have a look at just one of
these texts (collected by Alasdair Livingstone). It comes from the
house of a family of conjurer-priests at Assur, about 650 B.C., and
states the existence of three earths and three heavens. "At the Upper Earth he [the creator god] established the souls of men, in the
center; on Middle Earth, he made sit his father Ea, in the center"
(Ea is subterranean water); "in Nether Earth, he included the 600
gods of the dead *(Annunaki),* in the center." This makes three
levels in our world: the earth on which we live, then water be-

neath, just as Thales has it, and farther down, as the lowest register, the netherworld with its appropriate gods. Heaven has three corresponding levels too. The highest story belongs to the god Heaven, Anu, himself, together with 300 heavenly gods; Middle Heaven, made of resplendent stone, is the throne of Enlil, the ruling god; the lowest level, made of jasper, is the place of constellations: "he designed the constellations of the gods on that."[86]

From a Mesopotamian point of view, this sort of text apparently is meant to make religious tradition meet with the facts of the natural world in which we are living. The account still keeps to the form of cosmogonic myth: "the god made," established, included, designed, and sat down on his throne. Yet the result is a complete cosmos that could best be indicated by a drawing instead of a narrative plot. Livingstone states that these texts are "making existing theology accord more precisely with the facts of the natural world." Hermann Schibli said nearly the same about Pherecydes of Syros, the putative contemporary of Anaximander: "Pherecydes, in short, meant to provide an alternative version to the Theogony; he probably felt his own version more consistently and accurately explained the origin of the world and the gods of myth."[87] The Assyrian scholar, a "knowing one" from about 650 B.C., and the Greek author from about 540 seem to devote themselves to parallel efforts.

These ideas come quite close to those of the Presocratics, whose relation to Hesiod may be seen in a similar perspective. Pherecydes still spoke of gods, but altered their names to make them more meaningful: *Zas* instead of Zeus, alluding to "life," *Chronos*, "time," instead of Kronos.[88] Anaximander and Anaximenes, as far as we can see, no longer introduced gods' names, but preferred a neutral designation, "the Divine," *theion*. But Anaximander's system still recalls the three heavens of the Assyrian text. Tradition reveals that Anaximander spoke of heavens in the plural, which is very unusual in the Greek language and was partially misunderstood in the course of doxography.[89] Anaximander's original step was to assign three categories of heavenly bodies—stars, moon, and sun—to the three heavens; if this was inspired by Iranian lore, it still meant to "discover the argumentation *(logos)* about sizes and distances" in astronomy, as Eudemus, Aristotle's pupil, formulated.[90] Anaximenes improved on Anaximander by making the stars more distant than the sun; he said that they are fixed to a crystalline sky "like drawings," *zographemata*. This almost sounds like a translation of the Assyrian text: Enlil "designed" or "drew" the constellations on the heaven of jasper.[91] Another Akkadian text with astronomical content, *Enuma Anu Enlil*, has the same idea with a more theological coloring: "The gods designed the stars in their own likeness" on heaven; Peter Kingsley has pointed out that almost the same expression occurs in the Platonic *Epinomis* as a foundation of astral religion: the constellations are "pictures of gods, as (divine) images, fashioned by the gods themselves."[92]

The Assyrian text with the three heavens and Enlil's throne in the midst of them also evokes Ezekiel's vision of Jahweh on his throne, fixed to a wheeled chariot of complicated construction; "and the wheels went to and fro"; the throne is of lapis lazuli, with shining amber around it, just as at Assur.[93] The text of Ezekiel is dated at 593–2, thus coming between the Assyrian conjurer and Anaximander. Greeks at Miletus were anything but isolated. Anaximander, according to tradition, wrote just when Asia Minor was conquered by the Great King,[94] and Gyges had installed regular contacts with Nineveh more than a hundred years before that. The brother of the poet Alcaeus, a mercenary, had gone to Nebukadnezar's Babylon.[95]

What then is new about the Presocratics? What has made the distinction of "philosophy" as against mythical and rational speculations or wisdom literature? Eastern continuities, contacts, and prefigurations of Greek philosophy are manifest in many forms.

The Presocratics clearly knew and used the older traditions, at least as a kind of scaffolding.[96] No doubt their constructions were helped by this scaffolding, but some strange twists may also be attributed to it.

Still, it was nowhere else but in Greece that philosophy in the form we know came into being. It may be to the point to recall the different social situation of the Greeks—no kings, no powerful priests, and no houses of tablets, which meant more mobility, more freedom, and more risk for mind and letters.[97] In mathematics too the Greeks developed a new form of deductive proof in restructuring geometry.[98] A unique phenomenon comes into view with Parmenides, with his special form of conscious argumentation and proof.

Parmenides' famous paradox—that since "being is, not-being is not," there can be neither coming-to-be nor passing-away, neither birth nor death, for this would presuppose nonbeing—is a piece of self-contained argumentation. It seems to spell out Greek language, the Greek verbal system. Greek language has the marked contrast of aspects, the durative one, expressed, for instance, by *es-* (it is), and the punctual aspect, expressed for example by *phy-* or *gen-* (became), *physis, genesis.*[99] At the same time, however, and this is the really strange and surprising point, by this formula and its consequences Parmenides hits upon a principle which still dominates our physical worldview, the principle of conservation of the duality of mass and energy, as we express it today. Nothing can come from nothing, and nothing can completely dissolve or disappear; we cannot annihilate the smallest piece of refuse.

The language of older cosmogony still continues to resonate through the protest of Parmenides. Coming-to-be and passing-away, creation and annihilation, are established as modes of thinking in Mesopotamia and in Egypt just as in Greece.[100] In *Enuma Elish* the god Anshar is addressed: "You are of wide heart, determiner of destinies; whatever is created or annihilated, exists with you."[101] Thus even in Akkadian we find the three concepts of becoming or creating *(banû)*, destroying *(huluku)*, and being there *(bashû)* combined in a system which embraces and dominates everything. Yet the gods also speak to Marduk: "Command destruction and creation: it will be so."[102] In other words, *Enuma Elish* assumes that the god can simply command destruction or generation. This proves the ultimate power of the god, just as much later the Christian god, according to dogma, will create from nothingness. No, Parmenides protests, he cannot do so— and our understanding of science agrees with Parmenides.

Older cosmogonic speculation, transformed through the medium of Greek language by Parmenides, arrived at a new fundamental, that of "being," which is revealed by rational argument even beyond appearances. Later Plato introduced the basis of mathematics into the argument, the *a priori* concept—and until today we try to understand and to dominate nature by rational thinking with the aid of mathematical formalism. Parmenides insisted that meaningful language was directed toward "being," which also means toward truth in an absolute sense, beyond any personal, social, or political concern.[103] Philosophy has largely tried to follow such an ideal of truth. It threatens to become obsolete, though, with the onset of relativity and deconstruction within the more modern trends in the social sciences and humanities. It is still to be hoped that the Greek heritage will not be totally lost.

There is no reason to isolate the Greeks, but we continue to philosophize and even to think on Greek lines. Is it Eurocentric to insist, with Parmenides, that thinking and speaking should be adequate to "being"? Whether the Parmenidean principle of conservation in physics should be seen as an achievement within the "evolutionary theory of knowledge"[104] will not be decided here. The authority of wisdom which makes its point "just so" is disappearing. Questions and argumentation of philosophy will persist.

4

Orpheus and Egypt

Herodotus, the "father of history," has made us aware of the unique importance of Egypt for Greece. His book on Egypt has been the subject of thorough commentaries.[1] It is not the aim of the present study to review and resume this task; rather, we will take a look at pre-Herodotean and extra-Herodotean materials, some of which have only recently come to light and thus promise to enrich and to correct our picture. Nevertheless this exercise will lead back to Herodotus again and again. Religious contacts and interactions caught the historian's attention most of all, and these will mainly be in focus here, too. Of course it has to be acknowledged that modern scholarship has built up more extensive and more intimate knowledge of Egypt, its archaeological remains and iconography, its language and literature, and its spirit and peculiarities, than Herodotus could muster. Only a small sector of this vast panorama can be brought into view here.

After the breakdown of Assyria and the rise of king Psammetichus in Egypt (664–610 B.C.) Greek contacts with Egypt intensified, with Ionians from Asia Minor and islands such as Samos leading the ranks. Merchants followed mercenaries, trade flourished. The Ionians established a permanent settlement at Naukratis.[2] Under king Amasis (570–526) in particular the rela-

tions became closer. Herodotus writes of Polycrates, tyrant of
Samos, engaging in correspondence with the pharaoh and "sacri-
ficing" his ring (according to Egyptian wisdom) in order to im-
prove his luck (in vain).[3] At about that time an uncommonly successful potter at Athens bore the name Amasis, no doubt with
reference to the pharaoh—though it is left to us to speculate
whether he was an Egyptian himself or had just been given this
name by Athenian parents.[4]

Even earlier, Egyptian models had come to influence Greek
architecture, especially temple architecture[5] and monumental
sculpture. The so-called *kouros* figure, which makes its appearance in Ionia about 600, clearly reflects Egyptian art, down to the
position of the legs, even if nude statues soon look unquestion-
ably Greek, as do the temples.

It is more difficult to document interrelations in ways of thinking or religious belief. Still, some early indications of religious
syncretism come to mind. A Greek votive inscription from the
middle of the sixth century reads to "Zeus of Thebes,"[6] which
means that Amun, god of the capital of Upper Egypt, is identified with the Olympian Zeus by a person writing Greek. A little
bit later another Greek named Socydes applies his votive inscription to a bronze Apis bull, adding PANEPI which may be meant to
be an Egyptian designation for the "bull of Apis."[7]

More important is the relation between Dionysus and Osiris.
At first we may wonder what these two gods could have in common—the god of wine and ecstasy whom we have come to imagine mainly in the style of Attic sixth-century vase painting, and
the god of the dead, the primordial king who died. A fascinating
cult of the dead radiated from Egypt from ancient times, an at-
tempt to ensure life, even happiness, after death through complicated and costly ritual. The god at the center of this is Osiris,
who had been killed, buried, revived, and entrusted with rule of
the dead. Through rituals and formulas dead persons are trans-

formed to become Osiris and to arrive at divine life in the beyond. Greeks never adopted the whole of these mythologies and rituals, but they were impressed. Herodotus repeatedly states that Osiris is Dionysus; moreover, he is not the only one and hardly was the first to say so.[8]

By now we know for sure that Dionysus was not a new god in archaic Greece, for he had been worshipped and linked to Zeus already in the Bronze Age.[9] Worship had been continuous, it seems, on the Aegean islands and at Athens. If anyone would try to speculate about the origin of Dionysus, he would have to go far back into prehistory. The connection with Osiris, however, may have come about much later, possibly only in the sixth century B.C.

It is probable that the identification of Osiris and Dionysus antedates Herodotus. A fragment of Hecataeus (FGrHist 1 F 305) intersects with a chapter of Herodotus (2.156); it deals with the sanctuary of Buto in Egypt and introduces the goddess Leto and her son or foster son called Apollo/Horos. Hence Herodotus' story concerning Isis, Horos, and Seth (2.154.4 f.) must already have been in the book of Hecataeus. Seth, one character in this mythical drama, was always identified with Typhon, the antagonist of Zeus known from Homer and Hesiod; Pindar and Aeschylus refer to him in Egyptian contexts.[10]

Many Egyptian representations depict Osiris with vines and grapes. But this was hardly the essential link between the two gods. Two more peculiarities will strike the observer. Several Attic vase paintings from the second half of the sixth century present Dionysus arriving in a festive procession on a wheeled ship; in one of them the ship is carried on the shoulders of men instead, and this vase fragment was found in Egypt.[11] In Egyptian cults gods usually arrive in ships carried by men; ships on wheels are used in various Egyptian ceremonies too. It is not likely that the Greek vase painters had the idea of putting the Dionysiac ship on wheels independently from the older Egyptian practice, just about the time when Amasis had diplomatic relations with Samos.

At a certain Athenian festival, the identification of which has remained controversial, Dionysus appears in the form of a mask which is hanging from a pillar.[12] This is known from several groups of Attic vase paintings. The representation strangely resembles Egyptian Hathor pillars, which are found on Cyprus in the sixth century.[13] What cannot be explained from any Greek background is that quite a few of the Attic vase paintings show double masks hanging at the pillar and looking in opposite directions. Double masks of this kind are characteristic of Hathor pillars in Cyprus. Hathor is, among other things, a goddess of drunkenness and sexual energy. In the absence of texts the links with Dionysus cannot be spelled out further. But the closeness of iconography and possible ritual cannot be disregarded.

Beyond such Egyptian details that evoke Dionysus, one basic character of archaic Dionysus makes a fundamental connection with Osiris. From the end of the sixth century Dionysus is a god of mysteries, of secret initiation rites which are directed toward the afterlife and promise bliss to the dead beyond the grave. In that context another name is pertinent: Orpheus. This brings us to a controversy among Hellenists which has been going on for about 200 years, but which has been transformed quite recently by decisive new discoveries.

Orpheus, in Greek mythology, was a singer who charmed animals and went to the netherworld to bring back his wife, Eurydice. "Orphism" is a construct of religious history, a putative religious movement with Orpheus as a prophet and books of Orpheus as sacred texts. This particular worship has been a battlefield between rationalists and mystics since the beginning of the nineteenth century.[14] In the background was the question of how "classical" Classical Greece had been, or even whether the

Greeks ever had any serious religion beyond the flimsy tales of Homer, the rhetoric of Ovid, and philosophical allegories. Thus Orpheus emerged from the sphere of the opera, where he had been at home from Monteverdi to Gluck, to become the subject of intellectual and religious constructs pondering a lost and fascinating ancient religion. There was, first, the voluminous work of Friedrich Creuzer, who also paved the way toward a new appreciation of Dionysus; there was the immensely learned critical attack by Christian Lobeck, *Aglaophamus sive de theologiae Graecae mysticae causis* (1829), who found nothing in the evidence but popular banalities and late constructs. The "mystical" line was resumed by Johann Jakob Bachofen, who reconstructed from an Italiote vase "the doctrine of immortality of Orphic theology," *Die Unsterblichkeitslehre der Orphischen Theologie* (1867).

By then a new group of documents had appeared, gold plates found in tombs with texts about the afterlife. In 1836 the text of Petelia, near Croton in southern Italy, became known. It describes an impressive netherworld scenery of a white cypress, a forbidden spring, a Lake of Memory with guardians and a password to gain access. In 1879 excavations of two uncommon burial mounds at Sybaris/Thurioi, south of Tarentum,[15] brought to light texts which are the most suggestive to date, just because they keep part of their secret: "God you have become instead of a man"—"kid I fell into the milk." What does this mean?

The gold plates were termed Orphic from the start. Erwin Rohde, whose book *Psyche* gave the most thorough exposition of Greek beliefs about afterlife and of Dionysus (1894; 1898[2]), dealt with them; Albrecht Dieterich in Germany and Jane Harrison in England were also particularly fascinated by these texts.[16] Controversies, though, remained.[17] Wilamowitz wrote some devastating pages against Orphism; Ivan Linforth joined the minimalist trend.[18] Martin Nilsson tried to take an intermediate position. More recently, E. R. Dodds offered a brilliant exposition of the

critical attitude,[19] while Günter Zuntz voiced ultra-Wilamo-
witzian skepticism. Zuntz would not accept anything Dionysiac
or Orphic in the gold plates.[20]

New, decisive discoveries provided a new basis for the support
of Dionysiac or Bacchic mysteries, and hence for Orphism too.
The oldest of the gold plates so far, with the longest text, was
found at Vibo Valentia, ancient Hipponion, and was published
in 1974.[21] Its date is about 400 B.C.—no question about a dating
in the Hellenistic period or Late Antiquity.[22] Linguistic arguments point to Ionia for the origin of the texts and their possible
clientele.[23] The most startling finding was that the Hipponion
text speaks about *mystai* (initiates) and *bakchoi* (bacchants) on
their way in the netherworld; that is to say, it refers to Dionysiac
mysteries. For confirmation came the texts of Pelinna, in Thessaly, published in 1987. They proclaim that the dead person has
been "set free" by "Bakchios" and thus is guaranteed a new and
blissful life. The discoveries continued. A gold plate from Sicily,
very similar to the Hipponion tablet, was published in 1993; another one, from Pherai in Thessaly, appeared in 1997, with quite
a different text but equally with reference to Dionysus.[24] Gold
plates recovered from Aigion in Achaia and Pella in Macedonia
have little more than a name with the title *mystas*. There have
been recent discoveries at Sfakaki, Crete.[25] Another text, from
Lesbos, has been announced but remains unpublished thus far.[26]

In addition, graffiti-like writings on strange bone plates from
Olbia, Ukraine, were published in 1978.[27] They date from the
fifth century B.C.; their purpose or use is enigmatic. But on one
of them ΟΡΦΙΚΟΙ (last letter doubtful) can be read. The mother
city of Olbia was Miletus. Herodotus (4.76–80) reported a dramatic scene of Dionysiac mysteries occurring at Olbia. In other
words, there is no longer any doubt about the existence of Dionysiac mysteries and "Orphics" in the fifth century B.C.

Still more sensational is the papyrus of Derveni, found in 1962, incompletely published in 1982. Thanks to a colloquium held at Princeton in 1993, in collaboration with Kyriakos Tsantsanoglou, of Thessalonike, a more complete and corrected text is now available.[28] These are the relics of 26 columns of a papyrus scroll, preserved in a carbonized state at the pyre of a rich Macedonian tomb. The burial can be dated to about 300 B.C.[29] This is the only papyrus preserved in Greece so far, and it is one of the oldest literary papyri we have. It is unique in its content as well, for it presents a Presocratic commentary on the theogony of Orpheus.[30]

The gold plates and the Derveni papyrus have opened up two distinct perspectives on what may be called Orphism, the message of mysteries on the one hand, and philosophical speculation in book form on the other. Both sides are linked to the name of Orpheus, and both have to do with Egypt.

The new gold plates have provoked a host of studies, which are still going on.[31] Their context is now established beyond any doubt, thanks to the Hipponion text and especially to the Pelinna texts. The key words are *mystai* (initiates), *bakchoi* (performing ecstatic rituals of Dionysus), *telea* (ceremonies especially in the context of initiation), and "setting free." The Hipponion text says, addressing the deceased person: "You are going [along] a way on which others too, initiates and bacchants, are going, the holy way, in glory."[32] The dead person is imagined as proceeding on a sacred way amidst a community of bacchant initiates. To speak of Dionysiac mysteries is just to translate what is in the text.

The Pelinna texts give instruction to the dead person: "Tell Persephone that Bakchios himself has set you free." And the last line reads (with misspellings): "waiting for you, beneath the earth, are the ceremonies which the other blessed persons, too . . ."[33] These gold plates are cut in the form of ivy leaves.

When the Hipponion text was found, it was still uncertain

whether the word *bakchoi* referred to Dionysiac initiates or to ec-
statics in a more general sense. The Pelinna texts, however, dispel
all doubt as to *Bakchios:* he is Dionysus. The final verse of the
Pelinna texts refers to the "ceremonies" *(telea)* which are waiting
for the initiates "beneath the earth." The initiate *(mystes)* is in focus in the text from Pherai, too, which also alludes to the *thyrsos,*
the emblem of Dionysus.[34] We are dealing with documents from
Bacchic mysteries which are meant to guarantee a state of "bliss
beneath the earth" after death. Plato, in a well-known passage of
his Republic, refers to "purifying priests" who use books of Orpheus and Musaeus, and who deal with "gods who set free," *lysioi
theoi.* Even before Plato Pindar refers to "ceremonies which set
free of sufferings" *(lysiponoi teletai)* and thus guarantee bliss for
the dead. This gives a more general context to these gold plates,
beyond individual tombs.[35]

Günther Zuntz, in his thorough study, distinguished two
groups of gold plates, A and B texts. The Hipponion text clearly
belongs to the B group; the Pelinna texts have close affiliations
with A. Both groups, in spite of their differences, come from a
similar Bacchic environment. The date of the Hipponion tomb
attests that the cult goes back to the fifth century at least. The
documents from Crete go forward to the Roman imperial era.
No other Greek mystery cult provides comparable direct, personal documentation across so many centuries.

The reality behind these texts can be reconstructed with a high
degree of probability. To begin with, nothing points toward a
Bacchic or Orphic "church" with priests, dogma, and credo. As
Plato noted, the cult has itinerant "purifiers" and "initiators,"
kathartai, telestai, who, through the appropriate rituals, offer
their clients freedom from various afflictions, including the fear
of death and postmortal punishments. The key document for
such priests is a decree of king Ptolemy Philopator from Egypt,
dated at about 210 B.C., which orders "those who are performing

initiation rituals for Dionysus" to register at Alexandria.[36] They
are organized in "families," with tradition from "father" to "son"
and are presumed to guard a sacred text *(hieros logos)*, be it mythical stories or ritual formulas; this, the decree says, shall be deposited at the royal office in Alexandria under seal. That wandering
initiators would cover the distances between Macedonia, Thessaly, Lesbos, Crete, Sicily, and southern Italy is not remarkable. It
may be surprising that none of these documents has so far been
found in Attica; but here Eleusis was dominant, and Eleusinian
mysteries did not use such texts.

The most vivid picture is drawn by Plato, in the text about
beggars and seers already mentioned:

> [They] come to the doors of the rich and persuade people
> that they have the power, granted by the gods through sacri-
> fices and incantations, to make good with festivals and feasts
> for any unjust deed that happened because of this person or
> some ancestor . . . and they present a babel of books of
> Musaeus and Orpheus, the sons of the Moon or the Muses,
> they say, according to which they perform sacrifices; and
> they persuade not only private persons but whole cities that
> there is resolution and purification from unjust acts by
> means of sacrifice and merrymaking, for the living as well as
> for the dead; they call these *teletai* and claim that this sets us
> free from mischief in the beyond. But for him who does not
> sacrifice, terrible things are waiting.[37]

The author of Derveni too refers to certain people "who make
the holy things their craft" and offer the appropriate rituals but
give no proper explanation, he complains.[38]

The texts of the gold plates do not appear in classical literature,
as known by direct tradition. One can speak here of a kind of
subculture. But the classics throw out numerous hints and testi-

monies not only compatible with these documents but apparently alluding to them. Aristophanes, in his *Frogs,* brings to the stage a festive procession of initiates in the netherworld. No doubt he is referring to Eleusis, as the invocation of Iakchos, the mysterious god who leads the chorus, makes clear;[39] but the general idea of the continuation of the ecstatic festival after death is identical with the reference in the verse from Hipponion about the sacred way of initiates and bacchants in the beyond. Sophocles, in his *Antigone* (1118–1122), identifies Iakchos with Dionysus and makes him the Lord of Italy who rules also in the sanctuary of Eleusinian Demeter. Thus Bacchic mysteries of Italy in Hipponion style and Eleusinian mysteries are seen in perfect parallel. A poem by Posidippus of Pella (third century B.C.) expresses the wish: "May I reach in my old age the mystic way to Rhadamanthys," that is, to Elysium;[40] this would be the final destination of the sacred way evoked at Hipponion. A teacher at Rhodes is imagined becoming the "leader of mystics" in the beyond.[41] According to the Roman poet Accius, the regions of the netherworld are simply "mystic."[42] More important, and much older, are certain texts of Pindar. He describes in graphic detail the transmigration of souls, the judgment of the dead, and bliss in the beyond in his Second Olympian Ode (476 B.C.), dedicated to Theron of Akragas, and also in a Dirge (*Threnos,* fr. 129–131), and he refers to the bliss granted by the "initiations which set [a person] free from pain."[43] "Bakchios has set you free," the Pelinna texts proclaim more than 100 years later, and they promise "bliss beneath the earth together with the others." From another *Threnos* of Pindar, dedicated to an Athenian, the words resound: "He knows the end of life, he knows the beginning, granted by Zeus."[44] Here too the Pelinna texts give an impressive paraphrase: "Now you have died, and now you have been born, thrice blest, on this day."[45] From Theron's Akragas to fourth-century Thessaly the same ideas, the same hopes and promises are spelled out—

promises of Dionysiac mysteries. The gold plates are not a marginal curiosity but documents of a religious message that was widespread and well known even to the representatives of the literary elite.

It is true that the gold plates do not spell out the more special ideas which Plato has suggestively placed in the foreground: life as penitence, a secret guilt at the beginnings of humanity,[46] transmigration[47] as unimpeachable administration of justice. It is not the purpose of the gold plates to provide principles or systematic accounts; they serve the immediate aim of raising hopes for the individual, according to the professional engagement of purification priests. Common hopes may result in a common burial ground for believers. As a fifth-century inscription from Cumae in Italy states: "It is not allowed that anyone be interred here who has not become a bacchant."[48] The mystic experience turns into demonstrative privilege.

The texts are not just variations of one identical *hieros logos;* they present diverse ideas and outlooks. None is very precise as to the final destination of the dead. "I come as a suppliant to pure Persephone, that she should graciously send me to the place of the pure," some texts from Thurioi say.[49] Pindar too makes Persephone decide about the destiny of the dead (Fr. 133). "You will rule together with the other heroes," the text from Petelia predicts.[50] This promise might equally apply to Hesiod, Pindar, and Posidippus. Pindar has the perfect souls, tested thrice, travel to the tower of Kronos and the islands of the blest.[51] Posidippus alludes to Elysium, where Rhadamanthys dwells. "Go to the right, to the sacred meadows and groves of Persephone," one text from Thurioi says.[52] Is this the final destination, or is it Elysium, or else the "islands," even beyond these meadows? Some texts of Thurioi explicitly say: "You have become a god instead of a man."[53] But one should probably not generalize this special acclamation.

A wide, variegated, and long-lived complex of Bacchic mysteries is concerned with afterlife. Shall we call them Orphic? This question has remained open. Skeptics will contend that so far none of the gold plates bears the name of Orpheus. If Orphic-Bacchic has become a current term, this is based on a passage in Herodotus.[54] Arguments in favor of a role for Orpheus are attractive but inconclusive. The details of the netherworld's geography should come from an expert who has been there, and Orpheus would be uniquely qualified for this job. The doctrine of transmigration is best attested for Pythagoras; but a Bacchic connection does not point to Pythagoreanism.

The text from Pherai strikes a note of its own.[55] It begins with the word *symbola,* "password,"[56] and goes on to offer an artificial and complicated word plus the name of a goddess who is not very well known elsewhere; both words appear twice: ANDRIKEPAIDO-THYRSON–ANDRIKEPAIDOTHYRSON, BRIMO–BRIMO.[57] This sounds as if someone were presenting a password and repeating it for confirmation. The text goes on: "Enter the sacred meadow. The initiate is free from retribution." The meadow is a very ancient detail in descriptions of the netherworld; calling it sacred corresponds to the sacred way in the text from Hipponion. The remission from retribution recalls the declaration in texts from Thurioi. The word ANDRIKEPAIDOTHYRSON clearly is meant to be a riddle, not to be understood by the uninitiated. We might hear "thyrsos" (the Dionysiac emblem) in it and a vague "man and child" *(andri-, paid-),* which is easily associated with a scenario of initiation.[58] But the whole word also recalls Erikepaios, an enigmatic name of the primordial god from the rhapsodic theogony of Orpheus. The name first occurs in the so-called Gurob papyrus, a ritual text from the third century B.C.[59] It is hardly a coincidence that three other suggestive words of the Pherai text appear in this papyrus: *symbola, Brimo,* and *poine.* In consequence, one is inclined to name as Orphic both the mysteries at Pherai and those expressed in the Gurob papyrus.

This brings in the other set of evidence, the bone plaques from Olbia.[60] The context and use of these graffiti is still obscure; plaques of this kind were used for other notices too. The date, first half of the fifth century, is established by the lettering. The texts are striking. The word DION, which may confidently be taken as an abbreviation for Dionysus, appears several times; such abbreviations of gods' names occur frequently in graffiti from Olbia. One graffito has the suggestive sequence "life–death–life" *(bios thanatos bios)*, and in addition "truth" *(aletheia)* and, somehow written across each other, DIO once more, and ORPHIKOI. Another piece has "Peace–War, Truth–Falsehood" *(Eirene–Polemos, Aletheia–Pseudos)*, and DION again; a third has DION and *Aletheia*, and, in addition, "body–soul" *(soma–psyche)*. (The reading *soma* was added by Vinogradov in 1991.)

These are hints, allusions, suggestions, not really texts, but still significant pointers. The succinct sequence "life–death–life" in particular is poignant. The pronouncement of the Pelinna texts, "now you have died and now you have been born, thrice blessed, on this day," is nearly a commentary on these words, and they also recall Pindar's words about end and beginning of life[61] (Pindar is about contemporary with the Olbia graffiti). In addition, a form of thinking in opposites comes up, some sort of dualism which at once brings Heraclitus to mind. The insistence on truth as against falsehood is especially impressive. Heraclitus, however, was critical of "magi swarming at night, bacchants, initiates" who, in his opinion, "are initiated into conventional human mysteries in unholy fashion";[62] hence "Justice will condemn the architects and witnesses of lies."[63] Did Heraclitus condemn those very mysteries that are known at Olbia, the Milesian colony? The oldest description of rites of Dionysus Bakchios at Olbia is by Herodotus, just at the time of these bone plaques.[64] Skyles, king of the Scythians, "wished to be initiated to the worship of Dionysus Bakchios," which caused the Scythians to kill him. At Miletus Dionysus Bakchios rites are attested in the third century B.C. in a much-discussed inscription.[65] The oldest attestation for the Bacchic cry *euhai!*—variant *euhoi!*—comes from Olbia, inscribed on a mirror from a woman's tomb dating to about 500 B.C.[66] This exclamation would have an esoteric meaning for the persons involved in Bacchic rites, the *bebakcheumenoi*.

Another look at such rites is presented by Apulian vase paintings from the fourth century B.C. These vases again and again evoke Dionysiac bliss in the context of funerary monuments and funerary cult. Many of the vases were expressly made for the tombs, volute craters and the so-called barrel amphoras in particular; some have holes in the bottom and thus were unfit for normal use.[67] Standard scenes show Dionysiac ritual at the tomb, with grapes, tympani, ivy leaves; not infrequently a big ivy leaf is painted without pragmatic connection to the scenery. Ivy is the plant of Dionysus. The dead persons represented within the tomb monument get Dionysiac attributes too: thyrsus, *kantharos* (cup), and the typical basket *(kiste)* with ivy leaf. Striking additions are water basins, either beside the tomb or even within the tomb building, together with ablution pans which can be used for bathing, that is, pouring water over head and shoulders. Purification, tombs, and Bacchic scenery belong together.

One vase, which recently appeared on the market and is now at the Toledo Museum, Ohio,[68] depicts a unique scene: Dionysus himself, in Hades, is shaking hands with the god of the netherworld: ΗΑΙΔΑΣ, the inscription says. Dionysus is accompanied by maenads, with tympanum and torches, and a little Pan seems to be playing with Cerberus. Hermes, guide to netherworld passages, is present too. Shall we call Dionysus in such surroundings the Chthonic Dionysus, son of Persephone, who often was thought to be central in Orphism? His image here is not distinct from the normal god of the Bacchic *thiasos*. One myth says that Dionysus went down to Hades to bring back his mother,

Semele,[69] but she does not appear in this picture. This much is clear: Dionysus and his followers have no terror of the underworld. He is good friends with Hades and Persephone, and even Cerberus is no longer dreadful. We are reminded of a passage in Horace that has Dionysus going down to Hades, where Cerberus, like a friendly dog, licks his feet and thigh.[70] "Tell Persephone that Bakchios has set you free," this is the message told to the initiate in the Pelinna tablets: he or she knows the password of hospitality.

More popular in Apulian vase painting is the descent of Orpheus to Hades. There are several variants of a great canvas of the netherworld which have been known for a long time; a wall painting at Tarentum may be in the background.[71] Here Orpheus is seen playing his harp at the palace of Hades and Persephone, with all the infernal staff present: Tantalus, Sisyphus and Danaids, Erinyes, Medea's children, Heracles, and Cerberus. A hint of mysteries might be a group of persons with a blissful look but without mythological identity, "the happy family," as they have been called. Other representations of Orpheus may be even more telling in our context. The singer is shown amidst Thracians, but with water basins and incense stands, instruments of purification that make a strange presence among "barbarians."[72]

Another strange picture, unique in its iconography,[73] has a herm at the center and a young man with a lyre to the right who, surprisingly, is holding Cerberus on a leash, while from the left another young man and his old servant approach. No doubt the man with the lyre is Orpheus, even without a Phrygian cap, given other Apulian representations of this type. Thus at the borderline of life and death, marked by the herm, Orpheus controls the terror of the netherworld with his music.

More explicit is a vase painting known since 1974, displayed at Basel.[74] Here Orpheus is shown playing his lyre, not at the entrance of Hades' palace, but within a normal tomb building in front of an old, dignified man seated in the back; significantly, this man holds a papyrus scroll in his left hand. What must be called the Orphic hope for the afterlife could hardly be expressed more clearly: it is the song of Orpheus, contained in a book, which guarantees quiet happiness for the dead. This is the most direct testimony for an Orphic book we can expect in a picture. It is no use guessing which book the painter may have had in mind—the theogony of Orpheus, a commentary in the style of the Derveni book, rituals as in the Gurob papyrus, or a guide to the beyond of Hipponion type—no place can be assigned to it in *Orphicorum Fragmenta*.[75]

Of course it is impossible to reconstruct Orphic-Italiote afterlife beliefs from the iconography. The texts of Orpheus, the books that must have circulated, remain lost. We may still note that the presence of Orpheus characterizes just a small section of the vast corpus of Italiote vase painting. This does not encourage the claim that all funerary symbolism or even all funerary belief of Dionysiac or Bacchic character should be called Orphic. Orphism rather appears as one particular movement within a much broader and unspecific tradition of Bacchic cult and iconographic symbolism. The importance of books would anyhow point to the privileges of the upper class.

In short, incontrovertible evidence supports the fact of mysteries of Bacchic character, mysteries of Dionysus, with speculations about life and death and a message of bliss in the beyond. Indeed, "Orphics" probably celebrated at fifth-century Olbia. The testimonies start with the mirror from Olbia. They become explicit with the Olbia plaques and the Cumae inscription in the first half of the fifth century, are explicated by the Hipponion text about 400, and followed by all the other gold plates from the fourth century onward. The inscription from Miletus and the Gurob papyrus from Egypt confirm the mysteries, as do pertinent literary texts by Heraclitus, Pindar, Herodotus, Plato, Posidippus.

These mysteries are parallel to the Eleusinian enterprise, but they are not centrally organized; instead, itinerant initiators seem to have set them up. Hence they differ in the formulas of their message, and probably in ritual practice too. Still, there is a family resemblance that prevents us from construing totally separate groups with the evidence we have. The widespread use of Bacchic iconography confirms this idea: it was Dionysus who set the paradigm for how to speak and think about death, burial, and afterlife. If this largely became a fashion, it still radiated from the real existence of Bacchic mysteries since the sixth century B.C.

In the whole of this complex one detail points to a foreign and older origin. The gold plates of Hipponion type depict a scene where the dead person, suffering from thirst, arrives at the Lake of Memory; guardians at the lake insist on the password, which permits access to the water. This has always brought to mind a similar scene in the Egyptian Book of the Dead, including the picture that accompanies these texts:[76] we see a tree, a pond, and thirsty persons bowing to drink. For the Greek text the Egyptian illustration seems to be even more suggestive than the Egyptian formulas. At any rate the picture would make it easier for Greeks to grasp what this was all about. Without documentation for the details of cultural contact, we can just postulate that this would have happened in the first half of the sixth century. Suffice it to know that one important station of the netherworld pilgrimage described in the gold plates, the one detail preserved even in the short version of the Cretan exemplars,[77] derives from the main document of Egyptian funerary lore.

An intermediate link between Egyptian and Greek funerary symbolism is that of Phoenician silver plates, which are no less related to Egyptian funerary ideology. They were deposited in tombs but also carried as amulets. In these Phoenician monuments it is not texts that recall Egypt but pictures of gods of the solar route, "decans," of unquestionable Egyptian character.[78]

Thus we see that Egypt is taken to be the center of expertise for postmortal protection by various neighbors, in different ways but with common intent. This strengthens the argument that Greek Dionysus, as he shows up in funerary contexts, has undergone the spell of Egypt, and that Bacchic mysteries which claim to guarantee otherworldly bliss are influenced by the Osiris cult.

Whether these mysteries go back to the Bronze Age, as does the god Dionysus, or represent a comparatively recent development, attributable to cultural contacts since the seventh and sixth centuries, is much more difficult to decide. Even at Eleusis the mysteries proper, performed in a closed hall of initiations *(telesterion)*, establish their presence by special architecture only in the sixth century. It is tempting to see the interrelation of personal mysteries with what has been called the discovery of the individual in the archaic epoch. The likelihood is strong that the old and traditional cult of Dionysus took a turn toward concern with afterlife through the Egyptian impulse. As Herodotus has it,[79] after the original foundation of Dionysus worship some later "sophists" imported Egyptian lore afresh. In our words, Orphic-Egyptian Dionysus came to overlay and to transform Mycenaean Dionysus—this seems a plausible thesis after all, even if it cannot be proved in detail to the skeptic. Direct sixth-century evidence for the transfer is not to be expected.

In any case, the mysteries documented by the gold plates are not pure Egyptian lore. A few indications suggest the Iranian side;[80] this would point to the second half of the sixth century, when Ionia fell to Cyrus the conqueror. But a Hittite text too has been adduced for comparison.[81] A kind of syncretism would not be at all surprising. Itinerant magi and purifiers and initiators for Dionysus could well collaborate or borrow effective elements from one another; think of the much later but telling incident when Simon the *magos* wished to partake of the power of St. Paul (Acts 8:9–24).

*   *   *

The most important document for early Orphism, no doubt, is the Derveni book, carbonized remains of a papyrus scroll preserved from a funerary pyre in Macedonia. The tomb is from about 330–300 B.C.; the composition of the text may be dated to about 420–400 B.C.; the poem which the author is quoting must be earlier. The characterization of the text as "Presocratic commentary on the theogony of Orpheus"[82] does not cover the whole of the book; the first columns have some more general content. They are so fragmentary that interpretation will remain tentative at best, but they seem to deal with religious practice and with *magoi* in particular; Heraclitus is quoted by name, with two statements about the sun (B 3; B 67) known from before. The commentary on the poem of Orpheus starts only in the seventh column. A title *On Ceremonies (Peri Teleton)* would make sense.[83] The text is quoted in Philodemus' book *On Piety* and came to him via Philochorus and Apollodorus, apparently.[84] This proves that the Derveni text is neither exotic nor marginal, but part of the standard classical literature of the Greeks that could be read at Athens, too.

The fascinating Presocratic ideas of the Derveni author will not be analyzed here; he evidently leans on Anaxagoras and Diogenes of Apollonia, possibly on Leucippus/Democritus too. Nor will we be concerned with his theory and practice of allegory, through which he tries to transform Orpheus' grotesque mythology into a Presocratic worldview. It is the theogony of Orpheus itself, in the form of a hexametric poem, that commands attention. It is presented in quotations that often add absolutely new material to Orpheus text fragments. Orpheus' theogony, the dating of which has been so controversial, is now pushed back to the first part of the fifth or to the sixth century B.C.

The interpretation of the poem below presupposes that the Derveni author followed the hexameter text he had before his eyes, but that he did not feel obliged to paraphrase each verse; he may well have left out whole passages. This means that the reconstruction presented by Martin West with his usual expertise, which tries to deal solely with the fragments actually quoted, may be far from the original.[85]

Orpheus' poem begins with an appeal to secrecy and esotericism, a famous verse to which Plato too alludes: "Close the doors, uninitiated."[86] Then theogony begins. The first cosmic power that comes into being is Night, and she gives birth to Heaven: Heaven (Uranus) is introduced as the "son of night," and he "became the first king."[87] Here already Orpheus is in contrast to Hesiod, who makes Uranus the son of Earth (Gaia) and introduces Zeus' kingship much later. But it agrees with the testimonies of Aristotle and Eudemus: the Orpheus account starts from Night. Uranus as first king appears also in a famous text of Olympiodorus in which men are created from the soot of the destroyed Titans.[88]

The continuation fully agrees with Hesiod: "From him again," from Uranus, "Kronos, and then Zeus, the counsellor."[89] Kronos, in turn, committed a "great act" against Uranus and took kingship away from him (col. 14[10].5). No doubt a castration story is implied, as in Hesiod, though with different detail: the Orpheus text omits the birth of Aphrodite. In due course Kronos is succeeded by Zeus. Zeus "heard oracles from his father" (col. 13[9].1) and went to the "inaccessible sanctuary" *(adyton)* of Night, who gave him "all the oracles which afterwards he was to put into effect" (col. 11[7].10) "so as to establish his reign at Olympus" (col. 12[8].2).

The consequence of Zeus' hearing these oracles is startling: "He swallowed the phallus [of the king] who first had ejaculated the brilliance of heaven *(aither)*."[90] This at any rate is what the author understands, as he makes clear in his commentary. He is at pains to give a cosmogonic meaning to the scandalous sexual act and language; the genital, he says, represents the source of becoming in general, according to human knowledge; and it is meant to refer to the sun in this case, which is at the center of the world and of the universal god (col. 13[9]).

This translation and interpretation have been challenged. Both *aidoion* and *ekthorein,* the scandalous words, can have a different meaning in Greek. Martin West proposed to restructure the fragments quoted so that *aidoion* would become an adjective: "and the powerful *daimon,* the venerable, he swallowed, who first had jumped into the *aither.*"[91] The god who jumped into the *aither* would be Phanes, prominent in the later Orphic theogony, not Uranus. Yet this construct is contradicted by the text of the Derveni author: he clearly understands *aidoion* as "genital," and he quotes those words about the powerful *daimon* twice in a way that leaves no doubt about his syntax: "Zeus took into his hands the rule and the powerful *daimon.*"[92] Whatever we may think of the Derveni author, he was Greek, writing for Greeks about a text not at all unknown and available in its entirety. That he would play tricks of syntax and semantics to invent phallus and ejaculation is not plausible.

The myths of Orpheus were scandalous. Diogenes Laertius says in his proem that Orpheus "attributed to the gods repulsive acts which even certain people commit but seldom with the organ of speech." This clearly indicates "unspeakable" oral-genital contact, and thus proves that the author of Derveni is not alone with his fantasies. Swallowing a phallus is the very epitome of what Diogenes Laertios intimates.

"Jumped into the *aither*" seemed to be a satisfactory translation of the second part of the crucial verse, with an accusative of direction. Yet the beginning of the next column, which evidently keeps paraphrasing this very text, repeats the verb with another, more weighty and extensive accusative,[93] and thus leads us to believe that this is a direct accusative, linked to a transitive verb. The root of "jumping" *(thor-)* can have a sexual meaning, and it clearly has such in another quotation of the Derveni text; the transitive verb is attested in a fragment of Aeschylus, where it means "begetting monsters" by jumping. In the paraphrase of the Aeschylean verse, the lexicon of Hesychius introduces a pertinent verb *ekthorizo,* to mean "ejaculate"—which all our lexica fail to acknowledge.[94]

Going back to the start of this mythology, though, what is this phallus that Zeus is supposed to have swallowed?[95] The surviving text does not answer this question. But there has been castration, and the member did not fall into the sea, as Hesiod has it. The commentator goes on to say that the phallus, swallowed by the all-comprehending Air that is Zeus, is the Sun; the god "who first ejaculated Aither," the "most White and Shining one," must have been Uranus, Heaven. He created the brilliance of sky by a first ejaculation, before castration. It is consistent that Kronos is called the son of Helios (14[10].2).

Zeus swallowing the phallus of Uranus cannot be separated from the famous Hittite text about the Kingdom in Heaven.[96] This text has Kumarbi doing just the same to Anu, "Heaven." In consequence Kumarbi becomes pregnant with the Weather god, another god, and with the river Euphrates. And we find that Orpheus is following the Hurrite-Hittite model even here: in consequence of his dealings with the *aidoion,* Zeus now is carrying springs and rivers, together with all the other gods, in himself (col. 16[12]).

It has been generally accepted that the so-called succession myth, elaborated in Mesopotamia and Anatolia, somehow reached Hesiod. In Hesiod's version Zeus is not directly linked to the castration of Uranus. But even Hesiodic Zeus is a swallower; he swallows Metis, "cleverness," to have her at his disposal in his abdomen.[97] This is no less strange, even if we have got used to it on the authority of a "classical" text. The theogony of Orpheus proves to be closer to the old Anatolian, Hurrite-Hittite mythology than to Hesiod in this detail. This closeness is surprising, and

it may be why some classicists were glad to accept West's restructuring of the text; but neither the multiplicity of strands nor the
survival of curious details in later testimonies should be shocking.
In late Orphic fragments "Mother Hipta" makes her appearance,
acting as midwife at the birth of Dionysus from his father's thigh
and later as his nurse. Her name clearly preserves the old Anatolian Hurrite goddess Hepat, the consort of the Weather god, well
known to Hittites.[98] Here ancient Anatolian tradition enters right
into Orphic mythology.

If, however, it was the god of the beginnings, Uranus, who
"first ejaculated *aither*," this betrays a different, unequivocally
Egyptian line of tradition. In fact it belongs to the main line of
Egyptian cosmogonies. These start with an island rising from
Nun, the primeval ocean, and a first god taking his seat there,
Atum. In his loneliness Atum starts masturbating, and he ejacu-
lates Shu and Tefnut. Shu is Air, brilliant Air, Tefnut is his twin
sister; their children will be Heaven and Earth. The gross sexual
motif became a problem for the later Egyptians themselves. The
most direct formulations occur in pyramid texts, with later rein-
terpretations or alternatives, such as "spitting," for example.[99]
Shabako (715–701)—the first pharaoh of later Egypt whose name
is known to Herodotus[100]—had a statue erected which is inscribed with an old cosmogonic text, the so-called Monument of
Memphitic Theology.[101] The text mentions fingers and phallus,
besides the alternative images. Whatever the Egyptians' interest
in their cosmogony may have been at that time, such a monumental publication of cosmogony would not go unnoticed, and
it hardly was unique. The old theogony of Orpheus evidently
adopted striking details from such sources.

The continuation of the Derveni theogony proves to be no less
compatible with Egyptian beliefs. Zeus, after his act of swallowing, "has become the only one," carrying all the other gods with
him. These may be the most interesting verses of this theogony

(col. 16[12].3–6): "of the genital of the first-born king; from it grew, in addition, all the immortal, blessed gods and goddesses, and the rivers and lovely springs, and all the other things which had come into being then: but he himself became the only one."[102] This message about Zeus as unique is absolutely new, to be found only in the Derveni text. The phrase "he became the only one" *(mounos egento)* brings to mind the formula that became central later in Christian theology, *monogenes,* the "only-begotten" god. But the word already appears in Parmenides (B 8.4). Even more striking than the wording is the idea that "all the other gods" "grew onto him" *(prosephyn).* If we try to imagine this, we are drawn to Egypt again: in the sixth century, during the 26th dynasty, a fashion arose in Egyptian iconography of combining a plurality of gods in one grotesque figure. This is to express the theological idea of unity in multiplicity.[103] The text of Orpheus, as quoted in the Derveni papyrus, is the verbalization of this Egyptian idea of the composite god. There is nothing comparable in the early Greek evidence; the only reference is to other Eastern forms of speculation about composite gods, as it comes up especially in an Assyrian hymn.[104]

A corresponding passage appears in a later Orphic theogony, the Rhapsodies (OF 21a, cf. OF 167), evidently a remodeling of the passage quoted in the Derveni papyrus. Here Zeus is made to swallow Phanes, the first-born resplendent king, and thus "hides" everything within himself (OF 168). "Everything he has hidden, and brought it up again to the joyful light out of his sacred abdomen, realizing clever thoughts"; this includes, as another quotation says, "the rivers and the endless sea, and all the other things, all the immortal, blessed gods and goddesses, what had come into being then and what was to come later."[105] Clearly, the whole passage of the Derveni theogony is repeated here, with slight but significant variations. No composite god, no phallus, but still swallowing and bringing back a whole universe. The continuation in the later version expands the praise of Zeus to draw the picture of a world giant, with all parts of the world combined to build up a "macranthropus."[106] The composite god has come back in a new and more realistic form.

The continuation of the Derveni theogony needs only brief comment. A hymn to Zeus, which clearly was known to Plato,[107] follows the predication of a unique god. In it Zeus is called "the first and the last, flourishing with lightning, the head, the middle, and the conclusion of all, the king and ruler of everything."[108] This hymn is extant in two later versions, too, a shorter one quoted in Pseudo-Aristotle *De mundo* (401a25 = OF 21a), and a longer one, known to Porphyry (OF 168). Pseudo-Aristotle no doubt has the older text; whether this is identical with that of the Derveni author is unclear. The Aristotelian text contains additional verses which have left no trace in the Derveni papyrus. This piece of Orphic theogony might have gone through three stages: Derveni, Pseudo-Aristotle, and Neoplatonist. It is equally uncertain whether all the quotations of Orphic verses in Plato belong to the Derveni theogony.[109]

The god, who has become the only one, creates the world through thinking: "He thought out" *(mesato)*.[110] The parallel to Parmenides, who has his *daimon* "thinking out" Eros (B 13), is immediately apparent. But once more, so are parallels to Egypt. Look again at the Monument of Memphitic Theology: the text celebrates Ptah as the one who produces the gods "by heart and lips," that is, by thinking and speaking.[111] The ejaculation of air, the composite god, the creation by thinking—it is almost uncanny to find so many Egyptian particulars. But the evidence is clear.

The last preserved column seems to embark on a new theme, Zeus "joining in love with his own mother." This would lead to the birth of Persephone, according to later attested mythology, and then, by further incest, to the birth of Chthonic Dionysus, son of Zeus and Persephone. This Chthonic Dionysus, called Zagreus in the late epic by Nonnus, has been the very center of Orphic religion according to earlier theories of modern scholarship. Dionysus the child is declared king by Zeus. He takes his seat on the throne, but the Titans seduce him and he is killed, torn to pieces, roasted, and eaten; Zeus then kills and burns the Titans with his lightning, and from the rising soot men come into being. The main text is in the commentary on Plato's *Phaedo* by Olympiodorus, sixth century A.D.: "Four kingships are mentioned in Orpheus, first the kingship of Uranus, whom Kronos succeeded, cutting off his genitals; after Kronos Zeus became king, sending his father to Tartarus. Then Zeus was succeeded by Dionysus."[112] The Derveni text stops just short of this. The book, or at any rate the copy burned at Derveni, ceases after column 26; the rest of the scroll was left blank. We cannot know why the author stopped, or whether another volume was to follow. It is interesting that the Olympiodorus system of four kingships is fully compatible with the Derveni theogony, with Uranus as first king, but incompatible with the Rhapsodies, which have mysterious Phanes as king even before Uranus. Commentaries on Plato may have preserved the old version; radical skepticism as to the source of Olympiodorus, on the other hand, cannot be refuted either.[113] It is worth mentioning that certain much older texts make humans rise from the death of a rebellious god—Akkadian texts in fact, with *Atrahasis* and *Enuma Elish* leading the ranks.[114]

Dating the Orphic theogony was long controversial. Otto Kern argued for a date in the sixth century B.C.. We now see that the issue is not straightforward. We have evidence for at least two successive versions of the theogony of Orpheus, with common passages but also with contrasting motifs. Clearly, one theogony was available to an author writing about 400 B.C.. Since he drastically reinterprets the text by forceful allegorizing, the text itself, the original Orphic theogony, will have been considerably older.

This assumption is strengthened by the connection between Orpheus and Parmenides. Even before the Derveni discovery, some similarity was evident between the proem of Parmenides, riding through "the gate of the ways of Night and Day" to attain Truth, and Zeus in the Orphic texts, visiting the cave of Night to get cosmogonic information.[115] Now this episode is directly attested for the Derveni theogony (col. 10–13[6–9]). This suggests that Orpheus preceded Parmenides. In addition, the fact that one very original verse of Orpheus presents Zeus as "becoming the only one" gives support to the reading *mounogenes* in Parmenides (B 8.4), as against the alternative *oulomeles,* to characterize "being." This shows philosophy taking its cue from myth, and makes Parmenides dependent on Orpheus once more. And what has often been claimed to be an original idea of Parmenides, the ability of the goddess to create by means of thought (*metissato* B 13), finds its model in Orpheus (col. 23[19].4) too, with an Egyptian background. All this seems to confirm that Parmenides knew the poem of Orpheus, side by side with Hesiod. Accordingly, the Orphic theogony is firmly dated to the sixth century. This, however, is not the work that Proclus read and commented upon; to him we owe the bulk of *Orphicorum Fragmenta,* the Rhapsodies, which were a modernized version of the archaic text, expanded and changed in many ways. The old version must have been known to Plato, as it was to Aristotle and Eudemus. We do not know how long it was still available to be read by specialists. One quotation of the text in the Homeric scholia possibly comes from Crates of Pergamon.[116] One would expect to find traces of our text in Diodorus, who has much to say about Orpheus and Egypt. But he seems to use different sources, which are overshadowed in any case by Herodotus.[117]

There is hardly another field of Greek philology where so much new evidence has come to light in the last decades. Older accounts of Orphism are outdated. Even so, gaps and uncertainties remain. Further discussion and controversy will continue about the gold plates and especially about the Derveni papyrus, about the intention and role of that archaic poem of Orpheus, but also about the character and possible identity of the Derveni author. It is nevertheless clear that Orpheus brings together a host of older Eastern traditions, Akkadian, Hurrite-Hittite, and Egyptian most of all, traditions that are apt to enrich more than to obfuscate our picture of the Greek spirit.

In conclusion, let us get back to Herodotus and the much discussed text which is really the basis for the concept of an Orphic-Bacchic movement. Herodotus compares the Egyptian prohibition against the use of woolen garments in sanctuaries and for burial with Greek customs: "This agrees with what is called Orphic and Bacchic, but is (in reality) Egyptian and Pythagorean; for those too who take part in these rituals must not be buried in woolen garments."[118] "What is called Orphic-Bacchic" refers to certain rituals *(orgia)* that had to do with death and afterlife, with their appropriate taboos, and Herodotus has a thesis about origin and transfer.[119] The statement that these are Egyptian and Pythagorean can only mean that the taboo has been brought from Egypt by Pythagoras. That Egyptian ideas could be Pythagorean and Bacchic too has often been accepted. The role of Memory in the gold plates has been called a Pythagorean element.[120] In another passage Herodotus deals more extensively with the Egyptian origin of Dionysus cult.[121] There he postulates two successive phases of transfer, first by Melampus, with the phallus procession, later by certain "sophists" who brought more complete teachings *(logos)*. Is it possible to identify this later form as the Orphic impulse, more directly informed by Egyptian ideas, as against the Bronze Age cult of Dionysus? Herodotus does not give names, and we cannot even be sure that he knew for certain what he confidently puts into his account, but his suggestions generally do make sense.

5

The Advent of the Magi

With the fall of Sardis in 547 B.C., about one third of the Greek world suddenly became part of the Persian (Achaemenid) empire, and it was the leading section of Greece, in terms of development of economy, technology, art, and mind, that suffered this fate. The Persian domination lasted for more than 200 years, for six generations.[1] Not only did every Greek know what a *satrapes* was, but the title of "king," *Basileus,* was used as a proper name for the Shah of Persia. What was the result of such a long coexistence? None at all, some classicists tend to assume.

At the same time, many scholarly interpreters gladly notice the remarkable evidence for influence in the opposite direction, from Greece to the East. Greek sculptors were active in working out the reliefs of Persepolis, the new capital and ceremonial center of king Darius[2]; this is shown by style and confirmed by some inscriptional evidence. The Persian king also introduced coinage in the manner of Lydians and Greeks, at least for the western part of his empire; the golden coins of Darius with an image of an archer, the *Dareikoi,* were well known and coveted by the Greeks. As Horace expressed it much later (Epodes 2.1.156), something strange happened: "Conquered Greece conquered the uncivilized victor," *Graecia capta ferum victorem cepit*—or rather, *Ionia capta,* in this case. Yet the conquered could not remain indifferent to the victors. Influence from top to base, from the summit of power to the general populace, cannot have been absent.

The meeting of civilizations is a complex process. In this case Lydia, the Anatolian kingdom, should be taken into account as a link or messenger go-between. But our knowledge of Lydia, in spite of its protracted coexistence with Greeks, is extremely fragmentary.[3] Not even an indication of Lydian literature has survived. Lydia had first opened the way to Nineveh, at the time of Gyges, and it was the first conquest of Cyrus, the great king who broke out of Iran, the first block to build up his empire. Probably Sardis was the first model of a royal residence that came to the eyes of Cyrus. The temple of Artemis at Ephesus, which Croesus had begun to construct, was finished under Persian sovereignty. Cyrus' conquest of Babylon was to follow more than a decade later, in 535. It brought more splendor and made the Persian king successor to Assyrian-Babylonian kingship with all its ancient worldwide aspirations.

It is true that at that time, about 547 B.C., the Greeks had already arrived at a unique level of civilization. All the many Mediterranean peoples, and some beyond, had begun to adopt and to imitate Greek products and Greek fashion, be it sculpture, ceramics in black- and red-figure style, or the mythology illustrated in the vase paintings; but also the use of wine and the culture of the symposium in general—all this was spreading to the west, the south, and the north as far as Gaul and Germany. Ionia stood out and continued to lead in technology too, with the casting of big bronze figures, the building of a tunnel from two sides, the bridge across the Bosporus for Darius. Darius also ordered Skylax the mariner from Carian Caryanda to sail to India, and the sailor produced a description of the coast of the Aegean in a Greek book.

These examples show the interaction of Persian rule and Greek enterprise, and there must have been more of the kind. Yet after the great conflict of the Persian Wars, the Greeks seemed to form their self-conception from a tendentious contrast with other peoples. After 479, "Asia" was seen as the antagonist of "Hellas." Some Greeks were even prone to take Ionians for Asiatics. Consciousness of separation outweighed the common elements. It was this image of difference that was to make history.

The peculiar Greek perspective—which could also produce a counterperspective called the *mirage oriental* by critics—can only be set straight if non-Greek sources are available that show the other side. Surprisingly, to find and to use such sources proves more difficult and more complicated with the Persians than with Assyrians or Egyptians. Achaemenid tradition is not only quite fragmentary, but uncommonly complex. This calls for a special introduction.

Direct written evidence from the huge and long-lasting Achaemenid empire is incredibly meager. This is not a consequence of primitiveness but of progress. Just at this time the imperial administration definitely changed from clay tablets to leather scrolls, wooden tablets, and papyrus, with the use of Aramaic script and language. Sadly, the library of leather scrolls at Persepolis was destroyed when Alexander burned the royal palace there. But even without this act of vandalism, the new writing materials used in the empire had minimal chances of survival. As things stand, only Akkadian and Elamite cuneiform tablets and a few texts of cuneiform Persian remain in addition to the Greek and Hebrew accounts of the Achaemenid empire.

More than 1,000 "Persepolis tablets," written in Elamic, the language of Susa, have not yet been fully edited. These contain short receipts for goods or for money from everyday transactions, with many proper names, also names of gods; but this is not material from which one can construct history. Akkadian cuneiform texts of the Persian period come from the temples which were still functioning, but the Akkadians were not really interested in the Achaemenid empire. Among the few chronicles there is not one document about the Persian Wars or treaties with Greece. Another source is the small group of texts in cuneiform Persian, mostly inscriptions of the kings. Darius had a form of cuneiform developed to perpetuate his own achievements. It was used in the unique monument called "stand of the gods," Bagastana-Behistun, high up on a rock face, readable only by gods.[4] For the rest cuneiform Persian was hardly used; it could not compete with the alphabet.

Beyond these sources, there is the tradition of Old Iranian religion which still survives, with its own language and writings. This is Zoroastrianism or Mazdaism, the religion of Zarathustra. It has become rare; most Parsees live in Bombay, India, today. The corpus of their sacred writings is called Avesta. No doubt these are very old and authentic sources, but they present enormous difficulties to scholarly analysis.

Original texts may produce strange effects. Greek sources yield an ideal picture of "Zoroastres" as one of the ancient oriental sages, excelling in metaphysics, astrology, and magic. Italianized as Zarastro, he has become world-renowned through Mozart's *Magic Flute,* where he appears with a group of initiates to pronounce the principles of enlightened humanity. When the *Magic Flute* was first produced in Vienna in 1791, it was just twenty years after the authentic Zarathustra had come to be known in the Western world: Anquetil Duperron had brought, among other writings, a codex of the Avesta from Bombay to Paris and published it in 1771.[5] Those who read the translation were shocked. What nonsense, Voltaire groaned; no sublime wisdom there, just hardly understandable sentences and dull ritual from an absolutely foreign world. So much for authenticity. Still today, the friends of Zarastro will infinitely outnumber specialists in the Avesta.

What to make of these texts from a scholarly perspective? Are they related to the Achaemenid empire, and how? The religion of Zarathustra had its heyday in the epoch of the Sassanid reign, third to seventh century A.D. At that time it had the privilege of state religion; starting from the basic Aramaic, a special script was invented to fix the sacred scriptures in writing, with a very exact orthography for all phonetic details. This happened possibly about 400 A.D. Avestan is undoubtedly an old Iranian language with Indoeuropean grammar, cognate with cuneiform Persian and yet distinct. The root *arta-,* which means something like "order"—compare Greek *artios*—and appears in the names Artaxerxes and Artabanos, is *asha* in Avestan, where it designates one of the supreme divine powers. The Avestan language comes in two linguistic layers, an older and a newer one. The old form is mainly restricted to the "songs," the *Gathas.* These finally are taken to be original compositions of Zarathustra, or, the other way round, what we know about Zarathustra is what is in the *Gathas.* The newer Avesta consists of several parts, mainly a comprehensive liturgy, the *Yasna;* a book of hymns to single gods, the *Yashts;* and a "law against evil spirits," *Videvdat.* Among some shorter texts the *Hadoxt Nask* must be mentioned, the basic text about the fate of the soul after death.

The great and insoluble problem is chronology. There are no reliable dates at all for either the composition or the final written form of any of these texts. All the testimonies about the life and times of Zarathustra, be they Iranian or Greek, which range between 6000 and 550 B.C., are without probative value. Linguistics only provides a relative sequence: the *Gathas* are close to the Indian *Veda,* so the division between the Indian and the Iranian languages cannot be put back too much beyond the epoch of Zarathustra. Hence linguists have tended to date Zarathustra, that is, the *Gathas,* to about 1000 B.C. or earlier. Mary Boyce, an expert on Zarathustrians, has opted for this dating. Gherardo Gnoli, in contrast, has recently arrived at the date of 588 B.C. for

Zarathustra's ascendancy, on the basis of certain Persian sources.[6] As for the Avesta proper, it is common to assign it vaguely to the Achaemenid epoch, though the relation of the Achaemenid kings to the religion of Zarathustra turns out to be complicated and remains controversial. If we accept—what I think probable—that Ahura Mazda, "the Wise Lord of Living," is a name created by Zarathustra for the highest god, then Darius is a follower of Zarathustra, because in his cuneiform inscriptions the god who granted kingship to Darius is called by this very name, Ahura Mazda. King Artaxerxes II offered dedications to Mithras and Anahita, two divinities of Iranian tradition who do not appear in the *Gathas* but have their place in the collection of hymns, the *Yashts*. The name of Zarathustra—Greek *Zoroastres* or *Zaratas*—and some knowledge of his dual system, with an evil spirit, Angra Mainyu, opposing Ahura Mazda, is known to Greek writers in the fourth century B.C. Herodotus does not mention Zoroastres, but Xanthos the Lydian did.[7] Later the name shows up in Pseudo-Plato, *Alcibiades* (122a). The first important account of dualism is in Theopompus, as quoted by Plutarch; it is also discussed in Aristotle, Eudemus, and Aristoxenus.[8] Hence, at least from the Greek side, we are entitled to view the Avesta as parallel in time to late archaic and classical Greece. The written form may be much later—the *Gathas* were probably learned by heart. But no clear evidence exists even for the date of the final redaction of the Avesta during the Sassanid period, with its proper script. And only part of the Avesta corpus has been preserved.

No literature of the Sassanid epoch has survived, though this was a literate kingdom whose competing schools of philosophy and world religions all had their books. It was only after the Muslim conquest, in the ninth century A.D., that Zoroastrians composed a series of books which are still extant; these texts look back to the great times as they try to preserve the traditions. To mention just two titles: *Bundahishn* is a treatise on the origin of the world; the book of *Ardai Viraz* is an imaginative story of a journey to heaven and to hell. The language is Middle Iranian, called Pahlevi today; it uses Aramaic writing in a form that is idiosyncratic and often unclear; transcriptions may differ widely. There are few specialists in this field, and they do not always agree. Most of these writings were translated in the nineteenth century in the series *Sacred Books of the East,* directed by Max Müller, but these translations are not always reliable. New editions published in Bombay have limited circulation. Nevertheless these ninth-century books are more interesting in their content than Avesta liturgies; they also use parts of the Avesta that have since been lost. Hence specialists in the Iranian religion return again and again to these Pahlevi books to retrieve or reconstruct old and authentic Iranian traditions, even to find traces of non-Zoroastrian or pre-Zoroastrian Iranian religion. Richard Reitzenstein embarked on such studies, together with Heinrich Schaeder; Geo Widengren at Uppsala produced many detailed studies and comprehensive syntheses with this perspective and method.[9] This is fascinating, but such work necessarily skips over more than 1000 years with several fundamental revolutions of society and spirituality in between, marked by such names as Alexander the Great, Jesus, Mani, and Muhammad.

Back to archaic Greece. For the cultural interaction of Greeks and Persians before the great war, incontrovertible testimony comes from two words, *Megabyxos,* the title of the high priest of Artemis at Ephesus, and *magos,* a word that was to have a very special career.

The title of the Ephesian priest is known especially from Xenophon's *Anabasis;*[10] the testimonies continue down to Strabo. Xenophon uses the title as a proper name, as Greeks used the title of Basileus. Strabo says Megabyxos was a eunuch; his successor was selected by the administration in some foreign region and brought to Ephesus.[11] He was a person of unique distinction, who dominated the processions with elaborate dress and received a lavish funeral. Several paintings featuring the Megabyxos became famous.[12] Our literary texts usually write Megabyzos with a *z*, but one inscription, Latin texts, and etymology clearly favor Megabyxos, with the *x*. Megabyxos is a regular Persian name, *Bagabuksha;* the Greek-looking element *mega-* stands for the Iranian word *baga-*, god. One of the allies of Darius who helped the ruler usurp power from the *magos* bore this name, seen in the Behistun inscription and likewise in Herodotus.[13] He had a homonymous grandson who was active under Xerxes.[14] Since Justi's *Iranisches Namenbuch* (1895), *Bagabuksha* has been translated as "freed by the god," something like Greek *Theolutos;* but Benveniste has argued for an active meaning of the verbal root, "freeing the god," "giving joy to the god," or "serving the god."[15]

How did a Persian theophoric name get affixed to the priest of Artemis at Ephesus? We do not know the details, but this much is clear: when Croesus started to build the great marble temple at Ephesus, the priest cannot have had such a title. There must have been a new start, a new spirit and organization in that sanctuary after 547, when the Persians arrived,[16] either right away or under Darius, once he consolidated the Persian empire. The name appeals to god and to liberation: the priest, representing the Artemisium, would demonstrate a sacred status by his title, some form of liberty, impressive for those who understood Persian. Compare an episode from centuries later, when the representatives of another sanctuary, the *Galli,* priests of the Mother Goddess at Pessinus, came to meet the invading Romans "wearing their breastplates and images." They prophesied victory for the Romans and succeeded in securing their privileges.[17] That the great king of Persia was inclined to care for sanctuaries is shown by a letter of Darius, preserved in Greek in a late copy, which gives protection to the guardians of the grove of Apollo at Magnesia, even against the local satrap, "on behalf of the god who had revealed the full truth already to the ancestors."[18]

In such a way the priests of the Artemisium must have succeeded in securing their sacred privileges from the Persians. The title Megabyxos aimed to tell the Persians in their own language that they had to respect the Divine. This would guarantee the sanctuary's possessions and especially its right of asylum, possibly even freedom from taxes, as at Magnesia. Whether the Persians at once began to identify Artemis with their own Anahita, the "undefiled" goddess, is less clear. At any rate Ephesus profited from the catastrophe of Miletus (494 B.C.); Herodotus tells us that the King's Road started at Ephesus (5.54). The building of the temple continued, to be completed only after decades, around 500. Xerxes, during his war, ordered that the sanctuaries of Asia be burned, "with the exception of the temple at Ephesus."[19] Magi are presumed to have been present there in 356, when the temple was set afire; they grieved for this emblem of "Asia."[20]

An Iranian word that was to gain much prominence in Greek and European tradition is *magos,* which survives in the name and concept of magic. A special interest of Greeks in *magoi* in the fields of religion is marked already in Herodotus; Aristotle and his pupils refer to them too in the discussion of *barbaros philosophia.*[21] Critical scholarship in the nineteenth century, which carried a strong Enlightenment aversion against any magic, resulted in profound skepticism. The later traditions about magi were considered nothing but forgeries, such as Pseudo-Berossus, Pseudo-Manetho, Pseudo-Zoroaster—they were typical of late Hellenism and lacked historical value. Yet the story had begun much earlier.

The word *magos (magush)* is incontrovertible evidence for Iranian influence in Greece. Complication arises from its near absence in the Avesta and from its double meaning in Greek, referring either to Iranian priests or just to magicians in general.[22] The double meaning was already discussed in a book entitled *Magikos* attributed to Aristotle or Antisthenes.[23] The authentic magi, we are told, are priests with a special theology and ritual, to be distinguished from "the wizard's magic" *(goeteuktike mageia),* which means magic in the current sense. In fact the magi regularly occur in Herodotus as a class of Median priests, spokesmen of Persian religion in contact with the king. Themistocles, in his Persian exile, was said to have been instructed in the arts of the magi.[24]

As against the "authentic" magi mentioned from Herodotus to Aristotle, *magoi* in the other sense of itinerant magicians and sorcerers show up around the same time, notably in the Hippocratean treatise *On the Sacred Disease,* where they appear together with "purifiers, beggars, and quacks."[25] Here magi are mentioned first, the most prominent in such company. Somewhat similar references to magi are found in Sophocles[26] and Euripides,[27] and also in Gorgias' *Helena.*[28]

By common understanding, one turns to Heraclitus for the oldest mention of the word *magos;* for this very reason some editors of Heraclitus have suspected interpolation of this word.[29] But there is an older and more basic testimony which is usually overlooked, and it shows directly how the Greeks first met with this word. In the great Behistun inscription, king Darius, promoted to kingship by the will of Ahura Mazda, declares: "There was a man named Gaumata, a magus, who lied and spoke: I am Bardia,"[30] that is, the brother of Kambyses and heir to the kingdom. Every time the name Gaumata recurs in the course of the report, the epithet "the magus" is added, as if to make it unforgettable. The word is preserved in Old Persian, it is transcribed into Akkadian *(magusu)* and into Elamite *(makuis);* evidently it was an Iranian term not at home in the current bureaucratic languages. The text does not reveal what a "magus" is; it has the aura of an uncanny secret.

Yet the inscription does reveal that Darius sent "the same texts" to all his lands and gave order to read them to the public there (§ 70). This means that in every Greek city of Asia Minor, including the adjacent islands, the Behistun text was read at this time to the Greeks, the subjects of the king, in their own language, about 520 B.C. From then on the Ionians were acquainted with the word *magos,* and amidst the awe spread around the Persian king, the designation of his opponent must have gained a special fascination. As soon itinerant charismatics came around declaring "I am a magus," they would surely catch everyone's attention.

From the Iranian side, the word "magus" appears just once in the Avesta in an insignificant context.[31] But *magush* also shows up for religious functionaries in the Elamite tablets from Persepolis.[32] The relationship of Mazdaism, king, and *magush* in the period of the Achaemenids still remains difficult to define. But it is the Greek aspect which concerns us here. The corpus of Greek and Latin texts about magi, as collected by Bidez and Cumont, is very rich and variegated and cannot be analyzed here.[33] Authentic religious practice shows up at the borderline between Greek and Iranian, with a bilingual inscription of a man who was "magus for Mithras."[34] Tiridates king of Armenia, who came to Rome with a splendid retinue in 66 A.D. to do homage to Nero, was called *magus* by the Westerners and was believed to have "initiated" the emperor to participate in magical meals.[35] It may have been not much later that the homage of Eastern magi to Jesus the child at Bethlehem entered the Gospel of Matthew. Still later, in Sassanid state religion, priests of Zoroastrianism were again called *magi.*[36]

The text of Behistun, the inaugural document of the kingship of Darius, is also the basic evidence for the word *magos* in Greek. Very few other Greek texts remain from that time. Heraclitus probably wrote some 20 years later, and more than 80 years elapsed before Sophocles, Herodotus, and Hippocrates, the other authors referring to magi. In between there were the Persian Wars.

*   *   *

Iranian influence in fifth-century Greece may be sought in two areas of religious development: the idea of "heavenly immortality" together with a system of three heavenly tiers, and the principle of dualism in a universal world construct. In addition, remarkable amalgams of Presocratic ideas and magi theories demand interpretation, especially in view of a new source, the Derveni papyrus. Our discussion will omit topics of the god Time, the Iranian *Zurvan*,[37] and the Four Ages of the World,[38] famous themes that have had great resonance in earlier scholarship; they are totally dependent upon the ninth-century Pahlevi writings. Nor will we discuss Pseudo-Hippocrates, *On Sevens,* which was once judged sensational; it may be a mirage of reflections in later texts.[39]

The message that the dead will "ascend to heaven" is still widespread in the Christian tradition.[40] It first becomes dominant in Iranian religion and appears occasionally in fifth-century Greece. Is this specifically Iranian? The answer turns out to be complicated. Various parallels and similarities arise between the Greek and Iranian traditions, as well as independent developments.

Three general statements may safely be made. (1) The idea of going to heaven after death does not belong to the world picture that is common in Mesopotamia, Syria, Palestine, and Greece in, say, the beginning of the first millennium. Instead, the opposite idea usually prevails, that of a "land of no return" or a "house of Hades," which is a dreadful subterranean abode, a place of swamps and clay, without light, far away from the gods. "Let us sit down to weep" is the final message of the *Gilgamesh* epic; the quest for immortality has failed. No hope is left.[41] (2) The idea that the pious will ascend to god and rest with him forever is basic to the religion of Zarathustra since the earliest documents, the *Gathas.* (3) The idea of *psyche* or *pneuma* rising to heaven after death is found in Greece in scattered references beginning about the middle of the fifth century B.C., together with concepts of "spirit," *pneuma.*

The first statement does not need special documentation. As to the second, the classical document for the Mazdaic doctrine about the fate of the soul after death is the *Hadoxt Nask,* a text in the Avestan language.[42] The dead person, on the third night, will be met by his own "religion," *Daena,* in the form of a beautiful girl, who guides him in three steps, through good thought, good speech, and good deed, to the "lights without beginning," to the presence of Ahura Mazda. The passage is redescribed in the Pahlevi books, in *Bundahisn* and especially in the book of *Adrai Viraz.* There those three steps are specified as reaching the stars, the moon, and the sun, before ending at the "lights without beginning," in that order. Much earlier than the Pahlevi books are the texts of king Antiochus of Commagene, at the time of Augustus, who was celebrating the combined Persian-Greek tradition of his family in the lavish installations and inscriptions of his rock monuments at Nimrud Dagh and Arsameia. Here the body "will sleep, having sent the god-beloved soul ahead to the heavenly throne of Zeus Oromazes."[43] Already the *Gathas* mention the "abodes of blessedness, filled with light" which have been created for the wise, as the god gives immortality;[44] the passage for the believer is from good to better, from corporeal to spiritual, to the place where god is dwelling, who grants "salvation and not-dying in his realm."[45] "The house of praise, where the god went first, is promised to you."[46]

Some pre-Zarathustrian elements might remain in such formulations. "Immortal," *amrto-,* is an Indoeuropean concept, possibly linked to a drug ceremony, the *Soma/Haoma* cult, practiced long before Zarathustra and rejected by him. The Veda too tells of a heavenly paradise. Zarathustra teaches a clear polarity between corporeal and spiritual life in the *Gathas,* or, to be more exact, the life of bones versus the life of spirit, *ast-vant* against *manah-vant.* The Iranian terms echo in the Greek words for "bone" and "spirit," *ostoun* and *menos.* Whatever the date of Zarathustra and his *Gathas,* it will be much earlier than Plato and

Platonism. Interpreters of the Hellenic world in its archaic vigor loved to dwell on Greek corporality, not "broken" by the separation of "soul." Was some Iranian impulse instrumental in changing the outlook?

The gradual spreading of the idea of a heavenly abode of a *pneuma* or soul in the fifth century has often been documented and discussed. At times it has been termed a Pythagorean revolution,[47] which could be compatible with an Iranian connection. The evidence, however, is meager: two fragments of Epicharmus[48] and some passages of Euripides, two of which are from the 420s, *Erechtheus* and *Hiketides*. In the *Erechtheus* it takes the form of catasterism (transformation into stars). The girls sacrificed for the sake of Athens are transformed into the constellation Hyades. "I settled their *pneuma* in the *aither*," Athena says.[49] Does this mean that the person is split in two, that only a soul enters the heavens,[50] whereas the body belongs to earth? This was made the official message in the epigram for the dead from Poteidaia, 432 B.C.: "The air has received the souls, the earth the bodies."[51] The formulation is quite close to Presocratic ideas, with natural entities playing their proper role, and with the concept of return to the origins. The message also appears in verses of Euripides which the ancients took as a reflection of Anaxagoras: "Back goes" everything, earth to earth, "but what sprang from the generation of *aither*, has come back to the circle of heaven. Nothing dies of what has come into being."[52] Diogenes of Apollonia declared the soul to be immortal air and as such "part of the god."[53] We find a reflection of this even in Socrates, or at any rate in Xenophon's *Memorabilia* of Socrates.[54] The Platonic elaborations on this idea are familiar.

Is this Iranian lore, transmitted by the magi, or just an evolution of Presocratic speculation? Air and *aither* are typical concepts of Presocratic philosophy, as is the cosmogonic perspective on origins and return to origins. Zoroastrian texts have nothing comparable to this. In addition, precursors of such ideas originate in the Greek tradition. Heracles mounting his chariot to drive up to Olympus toward the gods is a favorite theme in sixth-century vase painting; but there is already seventh-century evidence for this ascent,[55] regardless of the interpretation of the verses in the *Odyssey* about Heracles in Olympus.[56] On the throne of Amyclae, according to Pausanias, Hyakinthus and Polyboia were shown "driving toward heaven,"[57] presumably in a winged chariot. If this is a sign of heavenly immortality, it would lead back even to the Minoan sarcophagus of Hagia Triada.[58]

Concerns with the afterlife must have come under Egyptian influence too, which was so strong in the field of funerary beliefs and funerary ritual.[59] Yet celestial immortality is not the message of Egyptian eschatology. Egyptians rather imagine the dead moving in the retinue of the Sun god through the realms of the netherworld to "go forth by day" again—this is the beginning of the *Book of the Dead*. The definite rising of a soul to heaven is closer to the Iranian than to the Egyptian paradigm. Likewise, the teachings of transmigration, normally credited to Pythagoras, were falsely attributed to the Egyptians by Herodotus; these most likely came from India, which was part of the Persian empire beginning with Darius. The Presocratic elements, on the other hand, the *aither* concept and the return to origins, could be typically Greek. In any case it appears that among Iranian, Egyptian, and Pythagorean elements, the intermingling of similar motifs and tendencies is too dense, and the determining contacts go back too far as against the extant Greek texts, so that a neat sorting-out of items and ways of transfer becomes impossible.

One indirect testimony does lead to an earlier period, perhaps to the earliest meeting of Greek and Iranian in this field: the world model of Anaximander, which corresponds to the ascent of the soul in three steps. Robert Eisler observed this resemblance in 1910, and I commented more fully on it in 1963.[60] The soul of the

Zoroastrian will reach first the stars, then the moon, then the
sun, and finally the "lights without beginning," where Ahura
Mazda dwells. The construct of heavenly rings or rather "wheels"
in Anaximander has the same sequence, with the smallest wheel,
next to the earth, assigned to the stars, the next to the moon, the
biggest to the sun, enclosed in the Infinite *(apeiron)*. This strange
entity, the Infinite, is "steering" everything, and it is called the
Divine. As an estimate of cosmic distances this is obviously
wrong; already Anaximenes introduced the correction that the
stars must be farthest away (A 7.6). Thus it is all the more plausible that Anaximander was not following natural observation
or intrinsic argument but religious speculation. That the sun, as
the highest of heavenly bodies, occupies the widest circle is an
idea that recurs much later in the speculations of Gnostics and
Mithraists.

   This cosmic vision has a wider context. Cuneiform texts of Assyrian priests proclaim three skies one above the other, with the
constellations fixed to the lowest one.[61] Ezekiel's vision depicts
the chariot-throne of Jahweh, the *merkavah,* with wheels full of
"eyes" whirling around.[62] A growing energy of cosmic speculation
seems to be on the move, from Assur and Iran to Jerusalem and
Miletus, beyond the borders of individual cultures. Anaximander
moves beyond Ezekiel, from religious vision toward astronomy,
in the differentiation of "wheels" and thus the gradation of distances; this had been in the Iranian message. We may accept that
Anaximander used Iranian lore for scaffolding[63] while proceeding
from soul to cosmos.

   More interesting and definitely more than disposable scaffolding is the principle of dualism. It is clear from the *Gathas* that
Zarathustra was a religious reformer who opposed older forms
of ritual, especially cattle sacrifice and *Soma* drinking, and who
changed the traditional terminology, indeed, reversed it. The old
Indoeuropean word for god, *deivos*—Latin *deus*—becomes the

designation of bad demons, *daevas,* whose worship is strictly forbidden. But the supreme god, called Ahura Mazda, has his antagonist, a principle of mischievousness, Angra Mainyu, the Bad Spirit. A persistent battle between the two powers is proclaimed, in which the pious find themselves inevitably engaged; they must take sides.

An elaborate account of this is found in *Bundahishn*—and much earlier in a modified, gnostic form in Manichaeism. But it is in Greek texts that we first encounter the doctrine in a datable context: Plutarch, in his book *On Isis and Osiris,* embarks on the problem of dualism, and for the Iranian doctrine he quotes Theopompus, the fourth-century historian; unfortunately, he does not indicate exactly how much he takes from this early writer. We learn about the attack of Angra Mainyu/Areimanios against the Wise God, about an intermediate period of battle, with periods of three thousand years each, and about the final victory of Ahura Mazda.[64]

Another relevant fourth-century text, preserved as a fragment, is by Aristoxenus.[65] He writes that Pythagoras went to Zaratas the Chaldaean, who explained that "from the beginning there are two causes for everything, a father and a mother: Father is light, Mother is darkness. The constituent parts of the light are hot, dry, light, and swift; particles of darkness are cold, wet, heavy, and slow. Out of these the entire cosmos is composed, female and male." This is much farther from the Iranian tradition than the quotation of Plutarch from Theopompus. It is not a translation, but a transformation of Iranian theology into Presocratic cosmology. The enumeration of opposites is nearly identical with Parmenides' *Doxa.* Aristoxenus claims that Pythagoras adopted this doctrine. The original doctrine of Zarathustra surely was different; its scope was theological and ethical, not cosmological. But the Aristoxenian provenance of the fragment should not be doubted, even if it shows a form of syncretism of Iranian and

Greek speculation. Zaratas is the Aramaic form of Zarathustra's name.

The third fourth-century account comes from a pupil of Aristotle's. Eudemus, in his survey of theologies, knows about various interpretations of the dualism of the magi:[66] the beginning is space *(topos)* or time *(chronos),* out of which "either a good god and an evil spirit have been separated, as some say; according to others . . . the primal duality is one of light and darkness. . . And the leader of one part is Oromasdes, of the other Areimanios." (This is the first clear transcription of the two fundamental names into Greek, Ahura Mazda and Angra Mainyu.) These doctrines and concepts were discussed in Plato's Academy and Aristotle's Lyceum. In his extant writings Aristotle mentions the philosophy of the magi just once: in opposition to the negative beginnings with Hesiod's Chaos or Orpheus' Night, they "make the first generating principle the best."[67] This would put Ahura Mazda above the "separation"—another interpretation of Iranian dualism.

People who pondered the question of influence of Iranian dualism on Greek philosophy mainly concentrated on whether Plato's construct of a bad world soul, as developed in the *Laws,* owes its inception to Zarathustra; Plutarch already asked this question in his book *On Isis and Osiris.*[68] Among moderns, Jula Kerschensteiner did the most thorough study of "Plato and the Orient." Her answer is negative.[69] But the question is bound to persist. It is not decisive for the interpretation of Plato as a whole, but for the history of ideas it would be essential to know more about the impact of concepts of this kind, just before the gate to the East was pushed wide open by Alexander. The information presented by Eudemus may well be attributable to this later stage.

But the first to teach a form of dualism in Greece was Empedocles, in the middle of the fifth century. Empedocles makes the antagonism of two principles the driving cause for natural processes. He names and describes these as gods, Love *(philia)* and Hate *(neikos);* the one is characterized as totally positive, sympathetic, and blissful, the other as negative, hateful, and destructive. Love creates life, Hate kills by separation. Empedocles tells a myth in this context, a combat tale about a battle regulated by predestined time: "But when Hate had grown big in the limbs (of *Sphairos,* the World as a perfect sphere of Being), he jumped up to reach for his honours, as time had come to its completion, which is marked out for them in alternation by broad oaths."[70]

Empedocles is quite an original creator of images and parables. But the system of the alternating powers of Love and Hate would not need such a dramatic tale, and the regulation by the "fullness of time" does not seem to reflect a scientific mind. Some modern interpreters of Empedocles tried to get rid of the cosmic periods of Love and Hate altogether. In another interpretation, Peter Kingsley presents Empedocles as a magician-doctor of Pythagorean tradition rather than a scientist and philosopher; through a fragment of Xanthus the Lydian which mentions Empedocles, he even construes some connection with the magi.[71] Gorgias spoke of Empedocles practicing magic, and Empedocles himself promises in his poem to perform miracles which are quite similar to what the Hippocratean treatise attributes to magi, beggars, and quacks.[72] That Empedocles met with magi is intrinsically plausible, even if no fragment of his can be found to prove it. If provisionally accepted, the thesis of such contacts will still not help much in interpreting Empedocles. But it would throw light on the situation during the fifth century, with Persia still looming large. One generation earlier, Persia had been the main stimulus in the career of another itinerant doctor, Democedes of Croton,[73] and one generation later, Ctesias of Cnidos became the personal doctor of king Artaxerxes II.

Magi as specialists for religious rituals make a new appearance in the Derveni book, in one column which became accessible only in 1997.[74] The Derveni text mainly deals with the theogony of Orpheus, pressing allegorical interpretations in the wake of Anaxagoras and Diogenes of Apollonia. But the first columns, which are more fragmentary than the others, make more general statements about *daimones* and souls. We read about Erinyes, who are "souls" (col. 2.5), about libations *(choai)* and "*daimones* from below." "They are called servants of the gods"; "they are [believed to be?] like unjust humans" (col. 3.6–8). Whether this was accepted, criticized, or denied by the author remains uncertain.[75] In the next column (4), Heraclitus is credited with two famous statements about the sun (B 3; B 67) and the Erinyes, who punish even cosmic transgression. Next, the "lack of belief" of certain people is criticized; "Disbelief and failure to learn are identical."[76] It seems that the author, in these introductory passages, is not concerned to refute religious practices and beliefs as absurdities, but to make sense out of them, possibly in a new way: "people are speaking correctly, but they do not know" what they are speaking about.[77]

Column 6 is the one that explicitly refers to magi. This is a line for line translation:[78]

(1) Prayers and sacrifices propitiate the souls. (2) The incantation of magi has the power to move the demons, who come in between as a hindrance, (3) from their place. Demons are a hindrance, (4) being enemies of souls. For this reason the magi perform the sacrifice, (5) as if giving atonement; and on the (6) sacred portions they offer libations of water and milk, from which they also make (7) the libations [for the dead]. Without number and with many nibbles (8) they sacrifice the cakes, because the souls too are without number. Initiates (9) make preliminary sacrifice to the Eumenides, in the same way as the magi. For the

Eumenides (10) are souls. For this reason one who is about
to sacrifice to the gods should (11) first [sacrifice] something
from a bird.

The text has gaps, with uncertain supplements, especially as regards the relation of *daimones* and souls in line 4.[79] In the larger
context, does the author wish to criticize or even ridicule the proceedings, or does he accept them by identifying *daimones* and
souls—which would have been a joy for Erwin Rohde and Jane
Harrison?[80] At any rate, we have a description both of rituals and
of explanations of these rituals from animistic principles. We find
magi as experts of ritual together with *logos,* explanation, which
takes account of demons and/or souls. Note the repeated formula: "for this reason" they know what they are doing.

The rituals deal with demons and souls rather than with gods.
They are effective by force of an incantation *(epoide).* Herodotus
too mentions an incantation of the magi at Persian sacrifices
(1.132.3). This incantation, the Derveni author holds, affects the
daimones. They are in the way for those who wish to contact the
gods; incantation removes the obstacles. In the next sentences
"souls" seem to come in with the same functions as *daimones.*
The rites are similar, though not identical, to the cult of the dead,
with libations of water and milk. The cakes with many nibbles, as
used in the cult, point to the multiplicity of souls: an object of
traditional ritual is given a special, perhaps a surprising sense.
The ultimate aim in all these actions must be to get into contact
with the god or gods. This is the function of sacrifice and prayer.
But this can be achieved only through the well-informed dealings
with the intermediate powers, as known by the magi.

The author states that the sacrificial practice of certain initiates
(mystai) resembles that of the magi; they act "in the same way,"
which does not mean identity. Initiates perform a preliminary

sacrifice to the Eumenides, who are souls—unfortunately such a sacrifice is not attested elsewhere in our evidence, neither for Eleusis nor for Samothrace nor for Bacchic mysteries.

The blood sacrifices of the magi have the character of atonement. Tsantsanoglou refers to the expression "I cut a sacrificial animal to offer atonement" in the Gurob papyrus.[81] Would this mean that such sacrifice is for demons only, not for the god of heaven? This would have parallels in Mesopotamia: first the demons must be satisfied, then the gods will come forth. To the sacrifices of the magi libations are added, an act of its own, but directed to the souls once more. This is compared with pouring libations *(choai)* in the cult of the dead, but also distinguished from that; both normal sacrifice and sacrifice at the tomb are considered. Greeks normally use wine for libation at the altar; pouring water and milk is a foreign detail. In Aechylus' *Persians* Queen Atossa pours milk, honey, water, and wine at the tomb of Darius (611 ff.). This is close to our text, but not identical.

It seems that the theme of souls and *daimones* induces the Derveni author to mention the magi. From our perspective, his indications of ritual and its meaning oscillate between an Iranian and a Greek view. Iranian religion, as it is known from the Avesta, features a complicated net of souls, ghosts, and demons. Clearly, more than two classes are distinguished; various terms identify pure and impure, benign and noxious powers. Experts may find correspondences with the Derveni text; it is quite improbable, though, that the incantation of the magi mentioned in this text could be found in a passage of the *Yasna* or *Videvdat.*[82]

From the Greek perspective, however, the insistence on the multitude of souls who are around everywhere leads to Presocratic doctrines. "The whole air is full of souls, they are believed to be *daimones* and heroes, and from them to humans the dreams are sent and the signs, and illnesses too." This is a sentence from the *Pythagorean Hypomnemata,* quoted by Diogenes Laertius.[83] It is a reinterpretation of the famous statement ascribed to Thales: "Everything is full of gods," or "of souls," or "of demons"—the quotations differ in this case.[84] A quasi-empirical confirmation is attributed to Pythagoreans, but also to Democritus: the motes which we see in a ray of sun falling into a dark room are souls.[85]

Of course the Presocratic perspective will transform souls into material entities. Diogenes of Apollonia made air, *pneuma*, the material and formative principle of the universe, especially of all living beings; a "piece of the god" is present in each of us, which is our soul.[86] The cosmic god, air, thus would include the totality of all souls. The Derveni author largely follows Diogenes: he calls the universe "Zeus" and considers it a *pneuma* that "rules everything."[87] In this sense the Derveni author could accept the doctrine of souls that are present everywhere, even if such a thesis originated in a different worldview. The author finds a new and profound sense in mysteries, as in the ritual of magi, and especially in the text of Orpheus. In this sense the first columns may be compatible with the main part of the text.

The magi of the new text evidently belong to the first category of the Aristotelian distinction: these are ritual specialists, not wizards. Their activities, as described here, have a close parallel in the text of Diogenes Laertius already quoted: "The magi deal with the veneration of gods, with sacrifices and prayers, because, they say, they alone are heard" by the gods.[88] This is independent of the Derveni text, but surprisingly similar, as it claims the magi's exclusive access to the divine through sacrifice and prayer. The reference to hindrances and their removal is peculiar of the Derveni text; that the magi will be heard by the gods is implied even there.

Diogenes Laertius goes on to state that the magi "also practice divination . . . [They say] that the air is full of specters, which flow by exhalation and penetrate into the sight of those who have sharp vision."[89] This brings back the multiplicity and ubiquity of souls or demons, yet in a strangely modern terminology. The word *eidola,* originally used for ghosts, had a special meaning in the theories of Democritus and Epicurus, which is reflected in Diogenes' text. The magi perceive flowing specters not through normal eyesight but through paranormal vision, be it of souls of the dead, of demons, or even of gods. Democritus, who had an elaborate but totally different mechanical conception of normal seeing,[90] developed his doctrine of *eidola*[91] for paranormal experience, for specters appearing at tombs, for dreams and visions. The text of Diogenes is full of Presocratic and later terminology, such as flowing *(aporrhoia),* exhalation *(anathymiasis),* penetrate *(eiskrinesthai).* This can have nothing to do with authentic Iranian priests; it must be Greek reinterpretation. Now the text of the Derveni papyrus comes as a surprising parallel, yet with much less modernization. It shows not only interest in the magi, but claims to understand and even to accept their teaching.

Taken together, the three texts discussed here—the Derveni passage, Diogenes Laertius with reference to Aristotle and Sotion, and the Pythagorean *Hypomnemata*—overlap in the doctrines about the omnipresence of souls or demons and their role in mantic visions. Twice practicing magi are singled out as representatives. We may take the ubiquity of gods, demons, and souls attending special sacrifices and mantic visions as the lore of practicing magi, transformed into *pneuma* physics by Diogenes of Apollonia, followed by the Derveni author, and adapted to atomic theory by Democritus. Even Democritus did not try to destroy traditional beliefs about souls and ghosts but established putative empirical evidence for them. From the perspective of Aristotle and his pupils looking back at the evolution of the doctrines, these might appear more similar than different, so that the magi were credited with the theory and even the terminology of Democritus. As yet the Derveni author had been immune to this transmutation.

The merging of magi, Diogenes of Apollonia, and Democritus is surprising but not unique. Herodotus, in a famous passage, writes that the magi venerate the circle of heaven as the highest god: "They sacrifice to Zeus, going up to the highest mountains; for they call the whole circle of heaven Zeus."[92] To what extent this agrees with authentic Zoroastrian Iranian religion is debatable. Ahura Mazda is a god of heaven, no doubt, but clearly conceived as a person in acting and reacting. Yet what Herodotus writes agrees perfectly with certain Presocratic positions—such as that of Diogenes of Apollonia, who takes air to be Zeus—and Euripides concurs, in the *Trojans,* staged in 415.[93] It is a chronological problem whether Herodotus could already have known Diogenes, or whether some earlier Presocratics had voiced a similar idea.[94] Most impressive is Democritus in a famous fragment: "Men endowed with speech *(logioi),*" he wrote "stretched up their hands to the region which we Greeks call 'air' now, and called the whole 'Zeus.'"[95] It is nearly the same in the Derveni text: "Since everything is called from that which is predominant, the Whole was called Zeus."[96] Here the Derveni author and Democritus are surprisingly close to each other. But, for Herodotus, Democritus' concept is the teaching of the magi. Herodotus and the Derveni author do not stand alone. It appears that many were prepared to see persuasive insights in the teachings of the magi, even if they were remodeling these teachings according to their own understanding and categories. Genuine Iranian lore is available not in fragments but rather amalgams, difficult to analyze. And probably we should not even insist on separating neatly what testifies to interconnections.

Many factors had to come together to create the so-called Greek Miracle. Not the least important was the fortunate aftermath of the classical epoch: Greek culture had the good fortune to find successors who established a heritage and took care of it continuously, while neighboring civilizations fell victim to the ravages of time and to the victory of either Christianity or Islam. This has created the mirage of a classical culture in isolation. Now that some knowledge of the lost civilizations has been regained, it is important to pay special attention to them. Let us try to see what was there before and around Hellenism, and not only celebrate singular achievements but spell out the results of interaction and dialogue in a continuing eastern Mediterranean *koine*.

Abbreviations

AHw	W. v. Soden, *Akkadisches Handwörterbuch*, Wiesbaden 1965–81
ANET	J. B. Pritchard, ed., *Ancient Near Eastern Texts Relating to the Old Testament*, 3rd ed., Princeton 1969
BWL	W. G. Lambert, *Babylonian Wisdom Literature*, Oxford 1960
CEG	P. A. Hansen, *Carmina Epigraphica Graeca* I, Berlin 1983
DK	H. Diels, W. Kranz, *Die Fragmente der Vorsokratiker*, Berlin ^{6}1951/ 52
FGrHist	F. Jacoby, *Fragmente der griechischen Historiker* 1923–.
KAI	H. Donner, W. Röllig, *Kanaanäische und aramäische Inschriften* I–III, Wiesbaden 1966–69^2
LIMC	*Lexicon Iconographicum Mythologiae Classicae*, Zürich 1981–1998
OF	O. Kern, *Orphicorum Fragmenta*, Berlin 1922
RE	*Pauly's Realencyclopädie der classischen Altertumswissenschaft*, Stuttgart 1894–1980
RlAss	*Reallexikon der Assyriologie*, Berlin 1932 ff.
RML	W. H. Roscher, ed., *Ausführliches Lexikon der griechischen und römischen Mythologie*, Leipzig 1884–1937
SAHG	A. Falkenstein, W. v. Soden, *Sumerische und Akkadische Hymnen und Gebete*, Zurich 1953
SEG	*Supplementum Epigraphicum Graecum*
SIG	*Sylloge Inscriptionum Graecarum* ed. W. Dittenberger, Leipzig ^{3}1915–1924
TUAT	O. Kaiser, ed., *Texte aus der Umwelt des Alten Testaments*, Gütersloh 1982–2001

Ancient Sources in
Various Translations

J. B. Pritchard, ed., *Ancient Near Eastern Texts Relating to the Old Testament*, 3rd edition with Supplement, Princeton 1969 (= ANET)

O. Kaiser, ed., *Texte aus der Umwelt des Alten Testaments*, Gütersloh 1982–2001 (= TUAT)

Sources Orientales I: La naissance du monde, Paris 1959. *Die Schöpfungsmythen*. Vorwort von M. Eliade, Einsiedeln 1964

MESOPOTAMIAN

Atrahasis: W. G. Lambert, A. R. Millard, *Atra-hasis, The Babylonian Story of the Flood*, Oxford 1969

    Bottéro-Kramer 527–564; Dalley 1–38

Gilgamesh: Das Gilgamesch-Epos übersetzt und mit Anmerkungen versehen von A. Schott, new edition, W. v. Soden, Stuttgart 1982

    A. R. George, *The Babylonian Gilgamesh Epic*, Oxford 2003

    ANET 72–99; Dalley 50–153

Enuma Elish: A. Heidel, *The Babylonian Genesis*, Chicago 1951²

    ANET 60–72; Bottéro-Kramer 604–653; Dalley 233–277

J. Bottéro, S. N. Kramer, *Lorsque les dieux faisaient l'homme. Mythologie Mésopotamienne,* Paris 1989

S. Dalley, *Myths of Mesopotamia*, Oxford 1989

B. R. Foster, *Before the Muses. An Anthology of Akkadian Literature,* Bethesda 1993

A. Falkenstein, W. v. Soden, *Sumerische und Akkadische Hymnen und Gebete,* Zurich 1953 (= SAHG)

W. G. Lambert, *Babylonian Wisdom Literature,* Oxford 1960 (= BWL)

D. D. Luckenbill, *Ancient Records of Assyria and Babylonia I–II,* Chicago 1926/7

M. Streck, *Assurbanipal und die letzten assyrischen Könige bis zum Untergang Niniveh's I–III,* Leipzig 1916

HITTITE

H. A. Hoffner, G. M. Beckman, *Hittite Myths,* Atlanta 1990

E. Neu, *Das hurritische Epos von der Freilassung I,* Wiesbaden 1996

EGYPT

A. Erman, *Die Literatur der Ägypter,* Leipzig 1923

M. Lichtheim, *Ancient Egyptian Literature I–III,* Berkeley 1973–1980

"Denkmal memphitischer Theologie": ANET 4–6; Lichtheim I 51–57; *Naissance* 62–64 / *Schöpfungsmythen* 83–85

IRANIAN

J. Darmesteter, L. H. Mills, *The Zend-Avesta I–III,* Oxford 1895; 1883; 1887 (The Sacred Books of the East 4; 23; 31)

H. Humbach, *The Gathas of Zarathushtra and the Other Old Avestan Texts* I, Heidelberg 1991

M. Boyce, *Textual Sources for the Study of Zoroastrianism,* Manchester 1984

A. Piras, ed., *Hādōxt Nask. Il racconto Zoroastriano della sorte dell'anima,* Rome 2000

BEHISTUN INSCRIPTION OF DARIUS

F. H. Weissbach, *Die Keilinschriften der Achämeniden,* Leipzig 1911, 8–74 (3 versions)

R. G. Kent, *Old Persian. Grammar, Texts, Lexicon,* New Haven ²1953, 116–134 (Persian version)

TUAT I 419–450 (all versions in German translation).

Bibliography

See also Ancient Sources in Translation.

Akurgal, E. 1968. *The Birth of Greek Art. The Mediterranean and the Near East.* London.

Aro, S., and R. Whiting, eds. 2000. *The Heirs of Assyria.* Helsinki (Melammu Symposia 1).

Assmann, J. 1990. *Ma'at. Gerechtigkeit und Unsterblichkeit im Alten Ägypten.* Munich.

Baurain, C. 1997. *Les Grecs et la Méditerranée Orientale. Des "siècles obscurs" à la fin de l'époque archaïque.* Paris.

Bernabé, A., and A. I. Jiménez San Cristóbal. 2001. *Instrucciones para el Más Allá. Las laminillas órficas de oro.* Madrid.

Bernal, M. 1987. *Black Athena. The Afroasiatic Roots of Classical Civilization.* Vol. I: *The Fabrication of Ancient Greece, 1785–1985.* New Brunswick.

Bianchi, U. 1976. *The Greek Mysteries.* Leiden (Iconography of Religions XVII 3).

Bickel, S. 1994. *La cosmogonie égyptienne.* Fribourg.

Bidez, J. 1945. *Eos ou Platon et l'Orient.* Brussells.

Bidez, J., and F. Cumont. 1938. *Les Mages Hellénisés.* Paris.

Bietak, M., ed. 2001. *Archaische griechische Tempel und Altägypten.* Vienna.

Boardman, J. 1964, 1999⁴. *The Greeks Overseas.* London.

———— 1990. "Al Mina and History." *Oxford Journal of Archaeology* 9, 169–190.

———— 1999. "The Excavated History of Al Mina." In Tsetskhladze, 135–161.

———— 2000. *Persia and the West. An Archaeological Investigation of the Genesis of Achaemenid Art.* London.

Bonnet, C. 1996. *Astarté. Dossier documentaire et perspectives historiques.* Rome.

Bonnet, C., and A. Motte, ed. 1999. *Les syncrétismes religieux dans le monde méditerranéen antique.* Rome.

Bonnet, C., and V. Pirenne-Delforge. 1999. "Deux déesses en interaction: Astarté et Aphrodite dans le monde égéen." In Bonnet and Motte, 249–273.

Borgeaud, P., ed. 1991. *Orphisme et Orphée.* Geneva.

Bottini, A. 1992. *Archeologia della salvezza.* Milan.

Bremmer, J. N. 1998. "Near Eastern and Native Traditions in Apollodorus' Account of the Flood." In *Interpretations of the Flood,* ed. F. Garcia Martínez and G. Luttikhuizen. Leiden, 39–55.

———— 2002. *The Rise and Fall of the Afterlife.* London.

Briand, P. 1996. *L'histoire de l'empire perse.* Paris.

Brisson, L. 1992. "Le Corps Dionysiaque." In ΣΟΦΙΗΣ ΜΑΙΗΤΟΡΕΣ. *Hommage à Jean Pépin.* Paris, 481–499 (= Brisson 1995, 481–499).

———— 1995. *Orphée et l'Orphisme dans l'Antiquité gréco-romaine.* Aldershot.

Brown, J. P. 2001. *Israel and Hellas* III. Berlin.

Budin, S. L. 2003. *The Origin of Aphrodite.* Bethesda.

Burkert, W. 1962. "ΓΟΗΣ. Zum griechischen 'Schamanismus.'" *Rhein. Museum* 105, 36–55.

———— 1963. "Iranisches bei Anaximandros." *Rhein. Museum* 106, 97–134.

———— 1967. "Das Proömium des Parmenides und die Katabasis des Pythagoras." *Phronesis* 14, 1–30.

———— 1968. "Orpheus und die Vorsokratiker. Bemerkungen zum Derveni-Papyrus und zur pythagoreischen Zahlenlehre." *Antike und Abendland* 14, 93–114.

———— 1972. *Lore and Science in Ancient Pythagoreanism.* Cambridge, Mass.

———— 1975. "Le laminette auree: Da Orfeo a Lampone." In *Orfismo in Magna Grecia*. Atti del XIV Convegno di Studi sulla Magna Grecia. Naples, 81–104.

———— 1976. "Das hunderttorige Theben und die Datierung der Ilias." *Wiener Studien* 89, 1–21 (= Burkert 2001, 59–71).

———— 1979. *Structure and History in Greek Mythology and Ritual*. Berkeley.

———— 1983a. *Homo Necans. The Anthropology of Ancient Greek Sacrificial Ritual and Myth*. Berkeley.

———— 1983b. "Apokalyptik im frühen Griechentum: Impulse und Transformationen." In *Apocalypticism in the Mediterranean World and the Near East*, ed. D. Hellholm. Tübingen, 235–254.

———— 1984. "Die orientalisierende Epoche in der griechischen Religion und Literatur." *Sitzungsber. Heidelberg Philos.-hist. Klasse* 1.

———— 1985. *Greek Religion*. Cambridge, Mass.

———— 1986. "Der Autor von Derveni: Stesimbrotos Περὶ Τελετῶν?" *Zeitschrift für Papyrologie und Epigraphik* 62, 1–5.

———— 1987a. "Oriental and Greek Mythology: The Meeting of Parallels." In *Interpretations of Greek Mythology*, ed. J. Bremmer. Beckenham.

———— 1987b. *Ancient Mystery Cults*. Cambridge, Mass.

———— 1991. "Homerstudien und Orient." In *Zweihundert Jahre Homer-Forschung* (Colloquium Rauricum 2), ed. J. Latacz. Stuttgart, 155–181 = Burkert 2001, 30–58.

———— 1992. *The Orientalizing Revolution. Near Eastern Influence on Greek Culture in the Early Archaic Age*. Cambridge, Mass.

———— 1994. "Orientalische und griechische Weltmodelle von Assur bis Anaximandros." *Wiener Studien* 107, 179–186.

———— 1995. "Lydia between East and West or How to Date the Trojan War. A Study in Herodotus." In *The Ages of Homer. A Tribute to Emily Townsend Vermeule*, ed. J. B. Carter and S. P. Morris. Austin, 139–148 = Burkert 2001, 218–232.

———— 1996. *Creation of the Sacred. Tracks of Biology in Early Religions*. Cambridge, Mass.

———— 1998. "Die neuen orphischen Texte: Fragmente, Varianten, 'Sitz im Leben.'" In *Fragmentsammlungen philosophischer Texte der Antike*, ed. W. Burkert, L. Gemelli Marciano, E. Matelli, L. Orelli. Göttingen, 387–400.

———— 2001. *Kleine Schriften I: Homerica*, ed. C. Riedweg. Göttingen.

———— 2003. *Kleine Schriften II: Orientalia*, ed. M. L. Gemelli Marciano. Göttingen.

*Cambridge Ancient History*² vol. III.2, Cambridge 1991; III.3, 1982.

Casadio, G. 1996. "Osiride in Grecia e Dioniso in Egitto." In P*lutarco e la religione*, ed. I. Gallo. Naples, 201–227.

Cassio, A. C. 1994. "ΠΙΕΝΑΙ e il modello Ionico della laminetta di Hipponion," *Annali dell'Istituto Universitario Orientale di Napoli* 16, 183–205.

Cornford, F. M. 1950. "A Ritual Basis for Hesiod's Theogony." In *The Unwritten Philosophy and Other Essays*. Cambridge, 95–116.

Dettori, E. 1996. "Testi 'Orfici' dalla Magna Grecia al Mar Nero." *Parola del Passato* 51, 292–310.

Dieterich, A. 1891. *De hymnis Orphicis*. Diss. Marburg.

———— 1893, 1913². *Nekyia*. Leipzig.

———— 1911. *Kleine Schriften*. Leipzig.

Dihle, A. 1970. *Homer-Probleme*. Opladen.

Dodds, E. R. 1951. *The Greeks and the Irrational*. Berkeley.

Dubois, L. 1996. *Inscriptions grecques dialectales d'Olbia du Pont*. Geneva.

Duchesne-Guillemin, J. 1996. "D'Anaximandre à Empédocle: Contacts gréco-iraniens." In *Atti del convegno sul tema: La Persia e il mondo greco-romano, Problemi attuali di scienza e di cultura* 76, Accademia Nazionale dei Lincei 368. Rome, 423–431.

Erskim, A. 2001. *Troy between Greece and Rome*. Oxford.

Fehling, D. 1994. *Materie und Weltbau in der Zeit der frühen Vorsokratiker. Wirklichkeit und Tradition*. Innsbruck.

Foti, G., and G. Pugliese Carratelli. 1974. "Un sepolcro di Hipponion e un nuovo testo Orfico." *La Parola del Passato* 29, 91–126.

Frel, J. 1994. "Una nuova laminella 'orfica,'" *Eirene* 30, 183–84.

Gebhard, E. R. 2001. "The Archaic Temple at Isthmia: Techniques of Construction." In Bietak, 41–61.

Giangiulio, M. 1994. "Le laminette auree nella cultura religiosa della

Calabria Greca: Continutià ed innovazione." In *Storia della Calabria Antica: Età italica e romana,* ed. S. Settis. Rome, 11–53.

Gigon, O. 1960. "Das Prooemium des Diogenes Laertios." In *Horizonte der Humanitas, Festschr. W. Wili.* Bern, 37–64.

Gnoli, G. 1984. "L'évolution du dualisme iranien et le problème zurvanite." *Revue de l'Histoire des Religions* 201, 115–138.

—— 1994. "Le religioni dell' Iran antico e Zoroastro; La religione Zoroastriana." In *Storia delle religioni* I, ed. G. Filoramo. Bari, 455–498; 499–565.

—— 2000. *Zoroaster in History.* New York.

Graf, F. 1974. *Eleusis und die orphische Dichtung Athens in vorhellenistischer Zeit.* Berlin.

—— 1993. "Dionysian and Orphic Eschatology: New Texts and Old Questions." In *Masks of Dionysus,* ed. T. H. Carpenter and C. A. Faraone. Ithaca, 239–258.

—— 1994. *La magie dans l'antiquité gréco-romaine.* Paris; trans., *Magic in the Ancient World.* Cambridge, Mass. 1997.

—— 1995. "Excluding the Charming: The Development of the Greek Concept of Magic." In *Ancient Magic and Ritual Power,* ed. M. Meyer and P. Mirecki. Leiden, 29–42.

—— ed. 1998. *Ansichten griechischer Rituale.* Stuttgart.

Guthrie, W. K. C. 1935, 1952². *Orpheus and Greek Religion.* London.

Guzzo Amadasi, M. G. 1967. *Le inscrizioni fenicie e puniche delle colonie in Occidente.* Rome.

Hackl, R. 1909. "Mumienverehrung auf einer rotfigurig attischen Lekythos." *Archiv für Religionswissenschaft* 12, 195–203.

Haider, P. W. 1996. "Griechen im Vorderen Orient und in Ägypten bis ca. 590 v. Chr." In *Wege zur Genese griechischer Identität,* ed. C. Ulf. Berlin, 59–115.

—— 2001. "Das Buch vom Fayum und seine Historisierung bei Herodot." In *Althistorische Studien im Spannungsfeld zwischen Universal-und Wissenschaftsgeschichte,* ed. P. W. Haider and R. Rollinger. Stuttgart, 127–156.

Harrison, J. 1903, 1922³. *Prolegomena to the Study of Greek Religion.* Cambridge.

Helck, W. 1979. *Die Beziehungen Ägyptens und Vorderasiens zur Aegäis bis ins 7. Jahrhundert vor Chr.* Darmstadt.

Heubeck, A. 1955. "Mythologische Vorstellungen des Alten Orients im archaischen Griechentum." *Gymnasium* 62, 508–525 = *Hesiod,* ed. E. Heitsch, Darmstadt 1966 (*Wege der Forschung* 44) 545–570.

Hölscher, U. 1953. "Anaximander und der Anfang der Philosophie." *Hermes* 81, 257–277, 385–418; rev. in *Anfängliches Fragen* (1968) 9–89.

Holzberg, N. 1992. Ed. *Der Äsop-Roman. Motivgeschichte und Erzählstruktur.* Tübingen.

Hornung, E. 2000. "Komposite Gottheiten in der ägyptischen Ikonographie." In *Images as Media,* ed. C. Uehlinger. Fribourg, 1–20.

Ivantchik, A. I. 1993. *Les Cimmériens au Proche Orient.* Fribourg.

Janko, R. 1984. "Forgetfulness in the Golden Tablets of Memory." *Classical Quarterly* 34, 89–100.

———— 2001. "The Derveni Papyrus (Diagoras of Melos, APOPYRGIZONTES LOGOI?); A New Translation." *Classical Philology* 96, 1–32.

———— 2002. "The Derveni Papyrus. An Interim Text." *Zeitschrift für Papyrologie and Epigraphik* 141, 1–62.

Jeffery, L. H. 1976. *Archaic Greece. The City States ca. 700–500 B.C.* London.

———— 1990. *The Local Scripts of Archaic Greece.* Rev. by A. W. Johnston. Oxford.

de Jong, A. 1997. *Traditions of the Magi: Zoroastrianism in Greek and Latin Literature.* Leiden.

Kearsley, R. A. 1999. "Greeks Overseas in the 8th Century B.C.: Euboeans, Al Mina and Assyrian Imperialism." In Tsetskhladze, 109–134.

Kern, O. 1922. *Orphicorum Fragmenta.* Berlin (= *OF*).

Kingsley, P. 1990. "The Greek Origin of the Sixth-Century Dating of Zoroaster." *Bulletin of the School of Oriental and African Studies* 53, 245–265.

———— 1992. "Ezekiel by the Grand Canal: Between Jewish and Babylonian Tradition." *Journal of the Royal Asiatic Society* III 2, 339–346.

———— 1995a. "Meetings with Magi: Iranian Themes among the Greeks, from Xanthus of Lydia to Plato's Academy." *Journal of the Royal Asiatic Society* III 5, 173–209.

———— 1995b. *Ancient Philosophy, Mystery, and Magic. Empedocles and the Pythagorean Tradition.* Oxford.

Klinkott, H., ed. 2001. *Anatolien im Lichte kultureller Wechselwirkungen. Akkulturationsphänomene in Kleinasien und seinen Nachbarregionen während des 2. und 1. Jahrtausends v. Chr.* Tübingen.

Koch, H. 1992. *Es kündet Dareios der König. Vom Leben im persischen Großreich.* Mainz.

Kopcke, G., and I. Tokumaru, eds. 1992. *Greece between East and West: 10th to 8th Centuries B.C.* Mainz.

Kotansky, R. 1991. "Incantations and Prayers for Salvation on Inscribed Greek Amulets." In *Magika Hiera,* ed. C. A. Faraone and D. Obbink. New York, 107–283.

Kristensen, W. B. 1992. *Life out of Death.* Louvain.

Kyrieleis, H. 1996. *Der große Kuros von Samos.* Berlin (Samos 10).

Laffineur, R., and R. Hägg. 2001. *Potnia. Deities and Religion in the Aegean Bronze Age.* Liège.

Laks, A., and G. W. Most, eds. 1997. *Studies on the Derveni Papyrus.* Oxford.

Lanfranchi, G. B. 2000. "The Ideological and Political Impact of the Neo-Assyrian Imperial Expansion on the Greek World in the 8th and 7th centuries B.C." In Aro and Whiting, 7–34.

Latacz, J., ed. 1991. *Zweihundert Jahre Homer-Forschung.* Stuttgart (Colloquium Rauricum 2).

Lemaire, A. 2001. *Nouvelles tablettes araméennes.* Geneva.

Lieven, A. v. 2000. "Die dritte Reihe der Dekane oder Tradition und Innovation in der spätägyptischen Religion." *Archiv fur Religionswissenschaft* 2, 21–36.

Livingstone, A. 1986. *Mystical and Mythological Explanatory Works of Assyrian and Babylonian Scholars.* Oxford.

Lloyd, G. E. R. 1979. *Magic, Reason, and Experience.* Cambridge.

———— 2000. "On the 'Origins' of Science." *Proceedings of the British Academy* 105, 1–16.

Lobeck, C. 1829. *Aglaophamus sive de theologiae mysticae Graecorum causis.* Königsberg.

Malkin, I., ed. 2001. *Ancient Perceptions of Greek Ethnicity.* Washington D.C.

Merkelbach, R. 1966. "Der orphische Papyrus von Derveni." *Zeitschrift für Papyrologie und Epigraphik* 1, 21–32.

Miller, M. M. 1997. *Athens and Persia in the Fifth Century B.C. A Study in Cultural Receptivity.* Cambridge.

Moeller, A. 2000. *Naukratis. Trade in Archaic Greece.* Oxford.

Momigliano, A. 1975. *Alien Wisdom. The Limits of Hellenization.* Cambridge.

Morenz, S. 1969. *Die Begegnung Europas mit Ägypten.* Zurich.

Morris, S. 1997. "Homer and the Near East." In *A New Companion to Homer,* ed. I. Morris and B. Powell. Leiden, 599–623.

Moscati, S., ed. 1988. *The Phoenicians.* Milan.

Murray, O. 1980, 1993². *Early Greece.* London.

Nilsson, M. P. 1952. "Early Orphism and Kindred Religious Movements." *Opuscula selecta* II, Lund, 628–83.

——— 1967³, 1961². *Geschichte der griechischen Religion* I, II. Munich.

Nissen, H.-J., and J. Renger, eds. 1982. *Mesopotamien und seine Nachbarn. Politische und kulturelle Wechselbeziehungen im alten Vorderasien vom 4.-1. Jahrtausend.* Berlin.

Obbink, D. 1994. "A Quotation of the Derveni Papyrus in Philodemus' On Piety." *Cronache Ercolanesi* 24, 111–35.

Oberhuber, K. 1977. *Das Gilgamesch-Epos.* Darmstadt (*Wege der Forchung*).

Osborne, R. 1996. *Greece in the Making, 1200–479 B.C.* London.

Papenfuß, D., and V. M. Strocka. 2001. *Gab es das griechische Wunder? Griechenland zwischen dem Ende des 6. und der Mitte des 5. Jahrhunderts v. Chr.* Mainz.

Patzek, B. 1996a. "Homer und der Orient." In *Vom Halys zum Euphrat. Thomas Beran zu Ehren,* ed. U. Magen and M. Rashad. Münster, 215–225.

——— 1996b. "Griechen und Phöniker in homerischer Zeit. Fernhandel und orientalischer Einfluß auf die frühgriechische Kultur." *Münsterische Beiträge zur antiken Handelsgeschichte* 15, 1–32.

Penglase, C. 1994. *Greek Myths and Mesopotamia. Parallels and Influences in the Homeric Hymns and Hesiod.* London; review by M. L. West, *Gnomon* 68 (1996), 657–662.

Pirenne-Delforge, V.. 1994. *L'Aphrodite grecque.* Liège.

Powell, B. B. 2002. *Writing and the Origin of Greek Literature.* Cambridge.

Prayon, F., and W. Röllig, eds. 2000. *Akten des Kolloquiums zum Thema Der Orient und Etrurien. Zum Phänomen des "Orientalisierens" im westlichen Mittelmeerraum (10.-6-JH. v. Chr.).* Pisa.

Pugliese Carratelli, G. 1993. *Le lamine d'oro "Orfiche."* Milan.

———— 2001. *Le lamine d'oro orfiche. Istruzioni per il viaggio oltremondano degli iniziati greci.* Milan.

Raaflaub, K., ed. 1993. *Anfänge politischen Denkens in der Antike.* Munich.

Reitzenstein, R., and H. H. Schaeder. 1926. *Studien zum antiken Synkretismus.* Leipzig.

Ribichini, S., M. Rocchi, and P. Xella, eds. 2001. *La questione delle influenze vicino-orientali sulla religione greca.* Rome.

Riedweg, C. 1996. "Orfeo." In *I Greci* II 1, ed. S. Settis. Turin, 1251–1280.

———— 1998. "Initiation–Tod–Unterwelt. Beobachtungen zur Kommunikationssituation und narrativen Technik der orphisch-bakchischen Goldblättchen." In Graf, 359–398.

Rohde, E. 1894, 1898². *Psyche. Seelencult und Unsterblichkeitsglaube der Griechen.* Freiburg.

Rollinger, R. 1993. *Herodots Babylonischer Logos. Eine kritische Untersuchung der Glaubwürdigkeitsdiskussion an Hand ausgewählter Beispiele.* Innsbruck.

———— 1996. "Altorientalische Motivik in der frühgriechischen Literatur am Beispiel der homerischen Epen." In Ulf, 156–210.

———— 1997. "Zur Bezeichnung von "Griechen" in Keilschrifttexten." *Revue d'Archéologie* 91, 167–172.

———— 2001. "The Ancient Greeks and the Impact of the Ancient Near East. Textual Evidence, and Historical Perspective (ca. 750–650 B.C.)." In Whiting, 233–264.

———— and M. Korenjak. 2001. "Addikritushu. Ein namentlich genannter Grieche aus der Zeit Assarhaddons (680–669 v. Chr.)." *Altorientalische Forschungen* 28, 325–337.

Roscher, W. H., ed. 1884–1937. *Ausführliches Lexikon der griechischen und römischen Mythologie.* Leipzig (= RML).

Rossi, L. 1996. "Il testamento di Posidippo e le laminette auree di Pella." *Zeitschrift für Papyrologie und Epigraphik* 112, 59–65.

Rusajeva, A. S. 1978. "Orfizm i kult Dionisa v Olvii [Orphism and Cult of Dionysus at Olbia]." *Vestnik drevnej Istorii* 143, 87.

Scarpi, P. 2002. *Le religioni dei misteri I: Eleusi, Dionisismo, Orfismo,* Fondazione Laurenzo Valla 2002.

Schefold, K. 1993. *Götter- und Heldensagen der Griechen in der früh- und hocharchaischen Kunst.* Munich.

Schibli, H. S. 1990. *Pherekydes of Syros.* Oxford.

Schmid, H. H. 1966. *Wesen und Geschichte der Weisheit. Eine Untersuchung zur altorientalischen und israelitischem Weisheitsliteratur.* Berlin.

Schmidt, M. 1975. "Orfeo e Orfismo nella pittura vascolare italiota." In *Orfismo in Magna Grecia, Atti XIV Convegno di Studi sulla Magna Grecia.* Naples, 105–138.

Schmidt, M., A. D. Trendall, and A. Cambitoglou. 1976. *Eine Gruppe apulischer Grabvasen in Basel.* Mainz.

Schuol, M. 2002. "Zur Überlieferung homerischer Epen vor dem Hintergrund altanatolischer Traditionen." In Schuol, Hartmann, and Luther, 331–362.

Schuol, M., U. Hartmann, and A. Luther. 2002. *Grenzüberschreitungen. Formen des Kontakts zwischen Orient und Okzident im Altertum.* Stuttgart.

Schwabl, H. 1962. "Weltschöpfung." RE Suppl. IX, 1433–1582.

Segal, C. 1990. "Dionysus and the Gold Tablets from Pelinna." *Greek, Roman, and Byzantine Studies* 31, 411–419.

Sommer, M. 2000. *Europas Ahnen. Ursprünge des Politischen bei den Phönikern.* Darmstadt.

Starr, C. G. 1961. *The Origins of Greek Civilization, 1100–650 B.C.* New York.

Stausberg, M. 2002. *Die Religion Zarathushtras. Geschichte, Gegenwart, Rituale.* Stuttgart.

Steiner, G. 1959. *Der Sukzessionsmythgos in Hesiods Theogonie und ihren orientalischen Parallelen.* Diss. Hamburg.

Strasburger, G. 1998. "Die Fahrt des Odysseus zu den Toten im Vergleich mit älteren Jenseitsfahrten." *Antike und Abendland* 44, 1–29.

Strommenger, E. 1962. *Fünf Jahrtausende Mesopotamien.* Munich.

Tsantsanoglou, K. 1997. "The First Columns of the Derveni Papyrus and Their Religious Significance." In Laks and Most, 93–128.

Tsetskhladze, G. R., ed. 1999. *Ancient Greeks West and East.* Leiden.

Uehlinger, C. 1997. "Qohelet im Horizont mesopotamischer, levantinischer und ägyptischer Weisheitsliteratur der persischen und hellenistischen Zeit." In L. Schwienhorst-Schönberger, *Das Buch Kohelet.* Berlin, 155–247.

Ulf, C., ed. 1996. *Wege zur Genese griechischer Identität. Die Bedeutung der früharchaischen Zeit.* Berlin.

Vinogradov, J. G. 1991. "Zur sachlichen und geschichtlichen Deutung der Orphiker-Blättchen von Olbia." In Borgeaud, 77–86.

Walcot, P. 1966. *Hesiod and the Near East.* Cardiff.

Wendel, C. 1949. *Die griechisch-römische Buchbeschreibung verglichen mit der des Vorderen Orients.* Halle.

West, M. L. 1966. *Hesiod, Theogony.* Ed. with Prolegomena and Commentary. Oxford.

—— 1971. *Early Greek Philosophy and the Orient.* Oxford.

—— 1978. *Hesiod, Works and Days.* Ed. with Prolegomena and Commentary. Oxford.

—— 1983. *The Orphic Poems.* Oxford.

—— 1985. *The Hesiodic Catalogue of Women.* Oxford.

—— 1988. "The Rise of the Greek Epic." *Journal of Hellenic Studies* 108, 151–172.

—— 1994. "Ab Ovo. Orpheus, Sanchuniathon, and the Origins of the Ionian World Model." *Classical Quarterly* 44, 289–307.

—— 1997. *The East Face of Helicon. West Asiatic Elements in Greek Poetry and Myth.* Oxford. Reviewed by K. Dowden, *Journal of Hellenic Studies* 121 (2001), 167–75.

—— 2000. "Fable and Disputation." In Aro and Whiting, 93–97.

West, S. 1994. "Prometheus Orientalized." *Museum Helveticum* 51, 129–49.

Whiting, R., ed. 2001. *Mythology and Mythologies: Methodological Approaches to Intercultural Influences.* Helsinki (Melammu Symposia 2).

Widengren, G. 1965. *Die Religionen Irans.* Stuttgart.

———— 1983. "Leitende Ideen und Quellen der iranischen Apokalyptik."
     In *Apocalypticism in the Mediterranean World and the Near East,* ed.
     D. Hellholm. Tübingen, 77–162.

Wiesehöfer, J. 1996. *Ancient Persia from 550 BC to 650 AD.* London.

Wilamowitz-Moellendorff, U. v. 1931/32. *Der Glaube der Hellenen* I–II.
     Berlin.

Wilcke, C. 2000. "Wer las und schrieb in Babylonien und Assyrien?
     Überlegungen zur Literalität im Alten Zweistromland." *Sitzungsber.
     Bay. Ak. de. Wiss. München,* 6.

Wirth, G. 2000. "Hellas und Ägypten: Rezeption und Auseinandersetzung
     im 5. bzw. 4. Jht. v. Chr." In *Ägypten und der östliche Mittelmerraum
     im 1. Jahrtausend v. Chr.,* ed. M. Görg and G. Hölbl. Wiesbaden,
     281–319.

Woodard, R. D. 1997. *Greek Writing from Knossos to Homer.* Oxford.

Wright, M. R. 1995. *Cosmology in Antiquity.* London.

Zhmud', L. 1976. "Die Goldlamelle von Hipponion." *Wiener Studien* 89,
     129–51.

———— 1992. "Orphism and Graffiti from Olbia." *Hermes* 120, 159–168.

Notes

Introduction

1. *Od.* 9.125–129.
2. *Od.* 1.3.
3. Cf. Bernal 1987; Burkert 1991; 1992.
4. See L. Poliakov, *Le mythe arien,* Paris 1971. Cf. n. 14.
5. R. Wood, *An Essay on the Original Genius and Writings of Homer,* London 1769.
6. E. Meyer, *Geschichte des Altertums* I–V, Stuttgart 1884–1902.
7. See Burkert 1991, 165 f.
8. W. Porzig, "Illuyankas und Typhon," *Kleinasiatische Forschungen* I.3 (1930) 359–378; E. O. Forrer, "Eine Geschichte des Götterkönigtums aus dem Hatti-Reiche," in *Mélanges Cumont,* Brussels 1936, 687–713.
9. F. Dornseiff, *Kleine Schriften* I, Leipzig 1959², 30.
10. H. G. Gueterbock, *Kumarbi. Mythen vom churritischen Kronos,* Zurich 1946; H. Otten, *Mythen vom Gotte Kumarbi, Neue Fragmente,* Berlin 1950; H. G. Gueterbock, *The Song of Ullikummi,* New Haven 1952.
11. See at n. 17.
12. T. B. L. Webster, *From Mycenae to Homer,* London 1958; D. L. Page, *History and the Homeric Iliad,* Berkeley 1969; C. H. Gordon, "Homer and Bible," *Hebrew Union College Annual* 26 (1955) 43–108.

13. Heubeck 1955.

14. Bernal 1987; he attacks traditional scholarship as racist because of its Western perspective. It is clear, however, that Egyptians and Phoenicians were neither Afroasiatic nor black—two among many details of Bernal's book that are open to expert criticism.

15. See Burkert 1992, 88–127, and, among more recent publications: Kopcke-Tokumaru 1992; Raaflaub 1993; Patzek 1996a and b; Ulf 1996; Rollinger 1996; Morris 1997; West 1997; Tsetskhladze 1999; Sommer 2000; Aro-Whiting 2000; Klinkott 2001; Whiting 2001; Papenfuß-Strocka 2001.

16. See also Malkin 2001.

17. The basic publication is M. Ventris, J. Chadwick, *Documents in Mycenaean Greek,* Cambridge 1956, 1972²; see F. A. Jorro, *Diccionario Micénico* I/II, Madrid 1986/1993.

18. Egyptian texts mention "sea peoples" harassing Egypt after 1200, among them the Philistines who settled at Palestine, which still bears their name; see T. Dothan, M. Dothan, *People of the Sea. The Search for the Philistines,* New York 1992. Some Mycenaens seem to have migrated to Cyprus by 1200 B.C.

19. Orientals took over the Greek name *Iawones* to designate Greeks in general: in Hebrew *Jawan,* in Akkadian *Iauna* (see n. 37). *Jawan* are partners of Tyre in Ezekiel 27.13. The Greek designation *Iawones/Iones* has a complicated history, which cannot be discussed here.

20. RE I A 2509. Text: Luckenbill II 36, § 70; the text of Assarhaddon about 12 kings of Cyprus, ibid. 261 § 690; R. Borger, *Die Inschriften Asarhaddons, Königs von Assyrien,* Graz 1956, 60 line 63–73.

21. A. Momigliano, "Su una battaglia tra Assiri e Greci," *Athenaeum* 12 (1934) 412–416 = *Quinto contributo alla storia degli studi classici e del mondo antico,* Rome 1974, 409–413.

22. See Ivantchik 1993.

23. See A. Ramage, P. Craddock, *King Croesus' Gold,* London and Cambridge, Mass. 2001. "Lud" as a partner of Tyre in trade (Ezekiel 27.10) could refer to Lydia.

24. Archilochus Fr. 19.1 West.

25. Main text in Streck 1916, 21 (*Annals* II, 95 ff.); successive elaborations of the text up to Gyges' death: Ivantchik 1993, 95–114; Burkert 2001, 229.

26. See Sommer 2000.

27. For Phoenicians on Rhodes, see J. N. Coldstream, "The Phoenicians of Ialysos," *Bulletin of the Institute of Classical Studies* 1 (1969) 1–8. A Phoenician silver bowl with Phoenician inscription has been found at Knossos, Crete. *Archaeological Reports* 1976/7, 11–14; Burkert 1992, 158, 3.

28. Burkert 2003, 252–266: "La via fenicia e la via anatolica. Ideologie e scoperte fra Oriente e Occidente."

29. See Burkert 1995. The "fable of the trees" in Callimachus Fr. 104, a clearly orientalizing piece (Burkert 1992, 121), is said to be Lydian.

30. See Pedon's monument n. 44.

31. London, Brit. Museum; Strommenger fig. 241; cf. J. M. Dentzer, *Le motif du banquet couché dans le Proche Orient et le Monde Grec du VIIe au IVe siècle*, Paris 1982. The pattern is copied in the well-known vase of Andocides, Munich, LIMC IV s.v. Heracles Nr. 1487.

32. Xen. *Anab.* 3.4.7–12. The name "Mespila" that was reported to him could mean "Lower City" in Semitic.

33. Phocylides Fr. 8 West, quoted by Dion Or. 36.13.

34. See n. 37; Haider 1996; Rollinger-Korenjak 2001.

35. Boardman 1964/1999; Boardman 1990; Boardman 1999.

36. R. A. Kearsley in Tsetskhladze 1999, 109–134 argues that Al Mina was a settlement of mercenaries rather than merchants. See also Burkert 1976 on Egyptian Thebes in Homer *Iliad* 9.382.

37. H. W. Saggs, *Iraq* 25 (1963) 76–78; Burkert 1992, 12; the situation seems analogous to Homer *Od.* 14.257 ff., Odysseus plundering in Egypt.

38. H. Kyrieleis, W. Röllig, "Ein altorientalischer Pferdeschmuck aus dem Heraion von Samos," *Mitteilungen des Deutschen archäologischen Instituts* (Athen) 103 (1988) 37–75; Burkert 1992, 16 with fig. 2.

39. See at n. 21.

40. See at n. 20.

41. V. Karageorghis, *Salamis. Recent Discoveries in Cyprus,* New York 1969, 23–150, "The Age of Exuberance." For the "sword with silver nails" corresponding to the Homeric formula, see Karageorghis 70, pl. 25.

42. Alc. Fr. 48; 350 Voigt; see W. Burkert, "'Königs-Ellen' bei Alkaios: Griechen am Rand der östlichen Monarchien," *Museum Helveticum* 53 (1996) 69–72.

43. Hdt. 2.152. Greek graffiti from Abu Simbel, about 589 B.C., SIG 1.

44. S. Şahin, *Epigraphica Anatolica* 10 (1987) 1 f.; O. Masson, J. Yoyotte, *Epigraphica Anatolica* 11 (1988) 171–179; SEG 37.994; 39.1266; early 6th century; it is unclear whether Psammetichus I (656–610) or Psammetichus II (595–585) is involved. For a similar monument from Kamiros, Rhodes, see Jeffery 1976, 356 nr. 10. See also *infra* Chapter 4.

45. Hdt. 2.178 f. See Moeller 2000.

46. Older than Aechylus' *Persians* is the elegy of Simonides on Pausanias and the battle of Plataeae, which has been recovered recently, Simonides Fr. 10–18 West². Simonides emphatically introduces the Trojan war as a paradigm of this conflict. See also Erskim 2001, 61 ff.

47. See Kyrieleis 1997; for the Nude Goddess, see Bonnet/Pirenne-Delforge 1999; N. Marinatos, *The Goddess and the Warrior: The Naked Goddess and Mistress of Animals in Early Greek Religion,* London 2000; for King Hazael's horse plates see n. 38.

48. See Bietak 2001.

49. H. G. Buchholz, V. Karageorghis, *Altägäis und Altkypros,* Tübingen 1971, Nr. 1267/8; Burkert 1977, 79.

50. Buchholz/Karageorghis 1971 Nr. 1740; 1741; Burkert 1977, 89.

51. E. R. Gebhard, "The Archaic Temple at Isthmia: Techniques of Construction," in Bietak 2001, 41–61.

52. See Papenfuß-Strocka 2001.

53. Cf. Burkert 1992, 21–25.

54. See Lloyd 2000.

55. See Sommer 1990, esp. 260–266. He underlines the growth of a "liberal" economy and the establishment of an oligarchy of merchants engaged in long-distance trade. Eastern craftsmen too sign their work, whether in Aramaic or cuneiform, see Burkert 1992, 16 n. 10.

1. Alphabetic Writing

1. A full-scale bibliography on the development of writing would outgrow the limits of this survey. Suffice it to refer to Jeffery 1961 and 1990; Heubeck 1979; Burkert 1992, 25–33; Woodard 1997; Powell 2002.

2. W. F. Albright, *The Proto-Sinaic Inscriptions and Their Decipherment,* Cambridge, Mass., 1966, has been supplemented by a few controversial findings.

3. M. Dietrich, O. Loretz, J. Sanmartín, *The Cuneiform Alphabetic Texts,* Münster 1995².

4. The name of the third letter, *gimel/gamma* is not clear: Akkadian *gamlu* "crook, boomerang," or "camel"?

5. See KAI; Sommer 2000, 207–209; 278–282.

6. See Wendel 1949; new documents in Aramaic from the Assyrian period in Lemaire 2001.

7. See Chapter V.

8. Woodard 1997.

9. See Burkert 1992, 25–33; Osteria dell'Osa, about 770 B.C., ευλιν or ενοιν: A. La Regina, *Scienze dell' antichità* 3–4 (1989–90), 83–88; A. M. Bietti Sestieri, *La necropoli laziale di Osteria dell'Osa,* Rome 1992, 209–212; E. Peruzzi, *Parola del Passato* 47 (1992) 459–68, and in *Civiltà greca nel Lazio preromano,* Florence 1998; D. Ridgway, in *The Archaeology of Greek Colonisation. Essays Dedicated to Sir John Boardman,* Oxford 1994, 42 ff; SEG 48, 1266, cf. SEG 48, 2101. The thesis of a much earlier adoption of the alphabet by Greeks is still upheld by some scholars, but it has to skip several centuries without any evidence.

10. Carian in Asia Minor is a special case, possibly connected with Southern Semitic.

11. See A. Abou-Assaf, P. Bodreuil, A. R. Millard, *La statue de Tell Fekherye,* Paris 1982, 39–42.

12. See Burkert 1992, 26.

13. Wendel 1949.

14. Dipylon jug: IG I² 919; Jeffery–Johnston 1990, 76 nr. 1; P. A. Hansen, *Carmina Epigraphica Graeca* I (Berlin 1983) nr. 432; SEG 48, 89; Nestor Cup: Jeffery–Johnston 1990, 239 nr. 1; Hansen nr. 454 (for the date, read 725–720 instead of 525–520); SEG 46, 1327.

15. Burkert 1992, 31.

2. Orientalizing Features in Homer

1. Burkert 1991, 155 f.; cf. Bernal 1987; Burkert 1992.

2. See Introduction at n. 3/4.

3. See at n. 28.

4. ANET 262–263.

5. Cf. Burkert 1991, 158 f.

6. A. Jeremias, RML II (189/97) 773–823 10; H. Usener, *Die Sintfluth-sagen,* Bonn 1899, 6–13; Usener's main object was to prove that the myth of the flood was Indoeuropean. For the various forms of the name Gilgamesh in cuneiform see H. Zimmern in Oberhuber 1977, 23.1.

7. W. E. Gladstone, *Homeric Synchronism,* London 1876; *Landmarks of Homeric Studies,* London 1890, Appendix; cf. n. 37 and Chapter 3 at n. 64.

8. C. Fries, *Das Zagmukfest auf Scheria,* Leipzig 1910; ZAG.MUK, or rather SAG.MU means "New Year."

9. H. Wirth, *Homer und Babylon,* Freiburg 1921; A. Ungnad, *Gilgamesch-Epos und Odyssee,* Breslau 1923, reprinted in Oberhuber 1977, 104–137; cf. Burkert 1991, 162–165.

10. G. S. Kirk, *Myth,* Berkeley 1970, 108; cf. Burkert 1992, 88 with n. 1.

11. See Introduction at nn. 27–41; Burkert 1992, 9–14. On Hittite texts and Homer see Schuol 2002.

12. See Chapter 1.

13. One item left is the name of Gilgamesh in a much later Aramaic text from Qumran, Burkert 1992, 32 f.; and "Gilgamos" shows up with a different tale in Aelian *Nat. An.* 12.21; RE VII, 1363 f.

14. A. Parry, ed., *The Making of Homeric Verse. The Collected Papers of Milman Parry,* Oxford 1971; A. B. Lord, *The Singer of Tales,* Cambridge, Mass. 1960, 2000²; see Latacz 1991; G. Nagy, *Homeric Questions,* Austin 1996; Morris–Powell 1997.

15. C. M. Bowra, *Heroic Poetry,* London 1952. See also Burkert 1992, 114–120; cf. S. Morris in Morris–Powell 1997, 599–623; West 1997, 164–275.

16. Burkert 1992, 115 ff.; West 1997, 220 ff.

17. Burkert 1992, 116; West 1997, 196–198.

18. *Gilgamesh* X.11 f.; Burkert 1992, 116; cf. Nergal and Ereshkigal (Sultantepe-Version) II 21', Dalley p. 167: "Ea . . . said to his heart."

19. Literally: "At the brightening of some of morning." Burkert 1992, 116; West 1997, 175.

20. Burkert 1992, 117; West 1997, 177–180.

21. Job 1.6; Psalm 82.1; 89.8.

22. Burkert 1992, 117; West 1997, 218 ff.

23. *Gilgamesh* I.206–299, only attested in the late version, that from Nineveh.

24. Wirth 1921, 112 f.; Burkert 1992, 117; West 1997, 403 f.

25. *Gilgamesh,* Old Babylonian version III.iv.141–148; Dalley p. 144; George p. 200 f.; Burkert 1992, 117 f.

26. *Iliad* 12.322–328.

27. *Gilgamesh* VI.162–163; *Iliad* 22.20; Burkert 1992, 118.

28. Lichtheim II 57–72.

29. Luckenbill 1926/7 II § 252–254; *Iliad* 20.498–501; Burkert 1992, 118f.; West 1997, 375 f.

30. OT Judges 4; Burkert 1992, 119.

31. Cf. H. Gese, *Die Religionen Altsyriens,* 1970, 54; Jeremiah 2.27; *Iliad* 22.126; *Od.* 19.163; Hes. *Theog.* 35; Burkert 1992, 119.

32. *Od.* 19.107–114; Hes. *Erga* 225–247; Streck 1916, II 6 ff.; Burkert 1992, 119.

33. Dihle 1970, 83–92.

34. Plato *Krat.* 402b; *Tht.* 152e; Arist. *Met.* 983b27; for other ancient quotations see West's edition of the *Iliad* II, Munich 2000, on Iliad 14.201. See also Burkert 1992, 91 with n. 10; West 1997, 147 f.

35. *Iliad* 14.201 = 302; 14.246.

36. *Iliad* 15.189, see at n. 57.

37. See n. 7; Hölscher 1953/1968; *Enuma Elish* I.1–5, Dalley p. 233.

38. Tethys appears as the consort of Oceanus in Hes. *Theog.* 337; 362; 368; Fr. 343.4; she is called a Titaness in Hes. *Theog.* 136.

39. Burkert 1992, 93; a phonetic problem remains; West 1997, 147 n. 20.

40. G. Bakir, *Sophilos,* Mainz 1981, 64 fig. 3; SEG 35, 37; Schefold 1993, 221 Abb. 229i; about 570 B.C. Oceanus and Tethys appear at the end of the gods' procession, i.e. in the position of "origin." This may be inspired directly by the *Iliad.*

41. Eudemus Fr. 150 Wehrli = Damasc. princ. I p. 322, 1.

42. See Dalley 1989, 229 ff.

43. Pirenne and Delforge 1994; Bonnet 1996; Budin 2003; for a possible Semitic etymology see M. L. West, *Glotta* 76 (2000) 133–138.

44. *Iliad* 14.214–217; Burkert 1992, 202 n. 18.

45. *Gilgamesh* VI.53–57; *Iliad* 14.315–328.

46. *Iliad* 15.36–38; *Od.* 5.184–186; Inscription from Sfire, ANET 659; Burkert 1992, 93 f.; 1996, 171.

47. Burkert 1992, 94 with n. 20.

48. Schefold 1993, 57 fig. 33; LIMC IV s.v. Hera nr. 202.

49. *Iliad* 14.274; 279; 15.225; 5.848; 8.478 f.; Burkert 1992, 94.

50. Burkert 1992, 94; Ebeling RlAss II, 396 f. s.v. Enmesharra: this god has fought Enlil and Ninurta and has been imprisoned in the netherworld, together with seven sons; *Enuma Elish* 4.111–128. See also F. Solmsen, "The Two Near Eastern Sources of Hesiod," *Hermes* 117 (1989) 413–422.

51. OF 114; Burkert 1992, 94; see ibid. 105–114 on a plausible link between the Akkadian epic about Erra and the Evil Seven with "Seven against Thebes" in Greek.

52. Burkert 1992, 38; 95.

53. ANET 99 f.; Lambert and Millard 1969; Dalley 1989, 1–38.

54. *Atrahasis* III.vi.10, p. 34 Dalley.

55. *Atrahasis* I.7–17; II.v.16–19, 30–33', pp. 80–83 Lambert and Millard.

56. *Atrahasis* tablet X, p. 116–119 Lambert and Millard.

57. *Iliad* 15.190–193; Burkert 1992, 89 f.; West 1997, 109–111.

58. Hes. *Theog.* 883–885.

59. *Atrahasis* III.vii.7 p. 35 Dalley.

60. *Atrahasis* I.352–359 = II.1–8.

61. Hdt. 2.117.

62. *Epicorum Graecorum Fragmenta* Fr. 1 Davies = Fr. 1 Bernabé.

63. Schol. AD *Iliad* 1.5; Davies p. 34–36; Bernabé p. 43 f., appendix.

64. Proclos, Davies p. 31; Bernabé p. 38.

65. Hes. Fr. 204, 95 ff. Merkelbach and West; West 1997, 480–482.

66. *Enuma Elish* I.29–54; 47; Dalley p. 234 f.

67. Burkert 1992, 103; Apollod. *Bibl.* 1.6.3, § 39–44.

68. W. Kullmann had declared the motif at the beginning of the *Cypria* to be pre-Homeric, without knowing about *Atrahasis:* "Ein vorhomerisches Motiv im Iliasproömium," *Philologus* 99 (1955) 167–192.

69. Schefold 1993, 127–129, Abb. 120a; LIMC s.v. Alexandros nr. 5 = Aphrodite nr. 1423 = Athena nr. 405.

70. *Iliad* 24.29.

71. See Introduction at n. 20; 41.

72. In *Gilgamesh* an assembly of the gods decides about the death of Enkidu; this scene is only extant in the Hittite version, Dalley p. 83 f.

73. Gilgamesh. VI 1–91, pp. 618–625 George.

74. *Iliad* 5.330–431; Burkert 1992, 96–98; West 1997, 361 f.

75. *Iliad* 21.505–513.

76. See n. 43.

77. Hom. *Hymn. Aphr.* 45 ff., 286–288; see RE I, 2107; RML I, 338.

78. Burkert 1992, 98 with n. 8. An Indoeuropean pedigree of *Diona* is assumed by G. Dunkel, "Vater Himmels Gattin," *Die Sprache* 34 (1988–90) 1–26. But names ending in *-one,* using a still active type of word formation, need not be aboriginally old.

79. *Gilgamesh* I.195–200, pp. 548–551 George.

80. *Gilgamesh* VI.53–57, pp. 620–624 George.

81. Burkert 1992, 82–87.

82. *Od.* 4.759–767; Gilgamesh III.37–45, p. 576 f. George; Burkert 1992, 99 f.

83. *Iliad* 16.220–252.

84. Women's rooftop ritual occurs in the Adonis festival, which is of Semitic origin; Aristoph. *Lys.* 389–396.

85. *Od.* 20.201 f.; W. Burkert, *Zum altgriechischen Mitleidsbegriff,* Diss. Erlangen 1955, 144–146.

86. BWL 190 f. (parody in the context of a fable); *Enuma Elish* I.45; Job 10.3; 10.8; Burkert 1991, 173 f.

87. *Atrahasis* I.27–102.

88. *Iliad* 1.396–406; Burkert 1992, 104–106; West 1997, 352.

89. J. Duchemin, *Prométhée. Histoire du mythe de ses origines orientales à ses incarnations modernes,* Paris 1974; S. West, "Prometheus Orientalized," *Museum Helveticum* 51 (1994) 129–149.

90. Burkert 1992, 39 with n. 30.

91. As against an 8th century date for Homer, a date in the 7th century seems to gain support, Burkert 1976; J. P. Crielard, *Homeric Questions,* Amsterdam 1993; M. L. West, "The Date of the Iliad," *Museum Helveticum* 52 (1995) 203–219. Contra, Powell 2002.

92. E. Reiner, "Die Akkadische Literatur," in W. Röllig, ed., *Altorientalische Literaturen,* Wiesbaden 1978, 157.

93. M. L. West, *Journal of Hellenic Studies* 108 (1988) 169: "Affinities with Near Eastern poetry . . . now clamour for attention from Homerists."

3. Oriental Wisdom Literature and Cosmogony

1. See Chapter 5 and below n. 18.

2. Arist. *Peri philosophias* Fr. 6 Rose; Fr. 35 = Diog. Laert 1.1, cf. 1, 6–11 = Sotion Fr. 36 Wehrli.

3. Damasc. *Princ.* 123–125, I p. 316–324 Ruelle = Eudemus Fr. 150 Wehrli; cf. Chapter 2 at n. 41.

4. Tatian 31; Clement *Strom.* 1.101 ff.; 5.89 ff.

5. Numenius Fr. 8 Des Places; cf. Aristobulus in Clement *Strom* 1.150.1.

6. E. Zeller, *Die Philosophie der Griechen in ihrer geschichtlichen Entwicklung* I⁷, Berlin 1923, 21–52; see also the "nota addizionale" by R. Mondolfo in E. Zeller, R. Mondolfo, *La filosofia dei Greci* I.1³, Florence 1959, 63–99.

7. A. H. Anquetil-Duperron, *Zend-Avesta. Ouvrage de Zoroastre,* Paris 1771. Cf. Chapter 5.

8. See Chapter 2 n. 7.

9. Cornford 1950.

10. Hölscher 1953/1968; Schwabl 1962; West 1966; Walcot 1966.

11. See K. Reinhardt, *Parmenides und die Geschichte der griechischen Philosophie,* Bonn 1916; M. Heidegger, "Der Spruch des Anaximandros," in *Holzwege,* Frankfurt 1950, 296–343; H. G. Gadamer, ed., *Um die Begriffswelt der Vorsokratiker,* Darmstadt 1968.

12. O. Gigon, *Der Ursprung der griechischen Philosophie von Hesiod bis Parmenides,* Basel 1945.

13. See at n. 66; Introduction n. 10.

14. Bernal 1987, see Introduction at n. 14.

15. A. N. Whitehead, *Process and Reality,* New York 1941, 63.

16. Cf. Chapter 1 and, for Greek epic, Chapter 2.

17. Anaximander A 7 DK.

18. Heraclitus A 1 DK = Diog. Laert. 9.6. See M. L. Gemelli Marciano, "Le contexte culturel des Présocratiques: adversaires et destinataires," in A. Laks and C. Louget, ed., *Qu'est-ce que la philosophie présocratique?,* Lille 2000, 83–114: 104 f.

19. Thales B 1/2 DK.

20. *Geographi Graeci Minores* I, 15–96; cf. K. v. Fritz, *Die Griechische Geschichtsschreibung* I, Berlin 1967, 52–54.

21. Hecataeus FGrHist 1; his map: 1 T 12 = Anaximander A 6.

22. FGrHist 2; 3.

23. Burkert 1972, 114–118.

24. Zenon A 1 DK = Diog. Laert. 9.25.

25. Burkert 1992, 41–46.

26. Ibid., 124 f.

27. J. Assmann, "Schrift, Tod und Identität," in A. and J. Assmann, Chr. Hardmeier, *Schrift und Gedächtnis,* Munich 1983, 64–93.

28. Hurrian wisdom literature has become accessible with the "Song of Liberation," Neu 1996. In general, see Schmid 1966; Uehlinger 1997.

29. An independent branch of Q ("Logien-Quelle," the reconstructed source of Jesus' sayings) has appeared with the gnostic Gospel of Thomas, Nag Hammadi II 2.

30. Now in evidence also in the Hurrite "Song of Liberation," Neu 1996.

31. Lichtheim I, 135.

32. W. Schmid, *Geschichte der griechischen Literatur* I, Munich 1929, 287 f.

33. See TUAT III 2 (1991) 320–347; Democritus B 299 DK (spurious?) = Clement. *Strom.* 1.69; Theophrastus Diog. Laert. 5.50, list of works nr. 273, p. 40 Fortenbaugh. The story of Achiqar has been reworked in the "Life of Aesopus," Burkert 1992, 32 f. with n. 30; Holzberg 1992; M. J. Luzzato, "Grecia e Vicino Oriente: Tracce della 'Storia di Ahiqar,'" *Quaderni di storia* 18 (1992) 5–84; "Ancora sulla 'Storia di Ahiquar,'" *Quaderni di storia* 39 (1994) 253–277.

34. Prov. 31.10; the "Babylonian theodicy" BWL 95.

35. Prov. 6.1–6; DK 10.34 and 11 A 2.

36. 10.3 § 6.1 DK; "A man is money," Aristodamus in Alcaeus Fr. 360 Voigt.

37. BWL 74 f.

38. Assmann 1990, 88; teachings of Amenemhotep, Lichtheim II 152.

39. Kleobulus 10.3 § 1 DK.

40. *Od.* 18.136 f.; BWL 40 f., 43, with an Accadian commentary, Burkert 1992, 118.

41. Archilochus fr. 196a West; W. H. Moran, *Harvard Studies in Classical Philology* 82 (1978) 17–19; Burkert 1992, 122 f.

42. See Assmann 1990.

43. Heraclitus B 94 DK; see Chapter 5 at n. 75.

44. Anaximander B 1 DK.

45. Parmenides B 1.11–14 DK.

46. Heraclitus B 30 DK.

47. Prov. 1.1–5.

48. Heraclitus B 1 DK.

49. See Sources in Translation.

50. Survey in *Sources Orientales: Naissance* or *Schöpfungsmythen*. For the "Monument of Memphitic Theology" see Chapter 4 n. 101.

51. See at n. 66.

52. Genesis 1 and 2.4 ff.: "Book of births" *(toledoth)* in 2.4 may be understood as title of the second part.

53. *Just So Stories for Little Children* were written by Rudyard Kipling, London 1902 (ff.); the title was taken as a polemical concept by E. E. Evans-Pritchard, *Theories of Primitive Religion,* Oxford 1965, 42, with reference to S. Freud's *Totem and Taboo.*

54. Anaxagoras B 1.

55. *Enuma Elish* I.1–8.

56. Pyramid text 1040 a–d, cf. 1466 b–d; *Sources Oriental: Naissance* 46.

57. Genesis 1.2; for the verb used in the text see L. Koehler, W. Baumgartner, Hebräisches und Aramäisches Lexikon zum Alten Testament, Leiden 1990³, 1137 f.

58. Hes. *Theog.* 116; the sense of *chaos* was very controversial already in antiquity.

59. Heaven the son of Night, *Ouranos Euphronides* Pap. Derveni col. 14; Arist. *Met.* 1071b27; Eudemus Fr. 150 Wehrli; see. Chapter 4 at n. 87.

60. Anaxagoras B 1 DK.

61. D. Tedlock, *Popol Vuh. The Mayan Book of the Dawn of Life,* New York 1985, 64.

62. Thales A 12 DK = Arist. *Met.* 983b20.

63. See Hölscher 1953/1968.

64. See Chapter 2 at n. 37.

65. W. Staudacher, *Die Trennung von Himmel und Erde,* Tübingen 1942 (repr. 1968).

66. Kumarbi: ANET 120, Hoffner-Beckman 40; cf. West 1966, 20–22; 211–213; see also Ullikummi: ANET 125, Hoffner-Beckman 59; Orpheus, see Chapter 4 at n. 89.

67. *Sources Orientales: Naissance* 47 § 9.

68. Anaximander A 1 DK. See also Leucippus A 1 § 32 DK.

69. See Steiner 1959.

70. Genesis 3.21.

71. Ptah: "Document of Memphitic Theology," Lichtheim I 52–56, *Sources Orientales: Naissance* 62–64; Marduk: *Enuma Elish* IV.22, "command to destroy and to recreate, and let it be so."

72. Xenophanes B 25 DK; for Orpheus, Parmenides, Egyptians, see Chapter 4 at n. 110/111.

73. See Chapter 4 at n. 110.

74. *Enuma Elish* IV–V, p. 254 f. Dalley.

75. Genesis 1.14.

76. Hes. *Theog.* 371–382.

77. Heraclitus B 123 DK. On *physis* see H. Patzer, *Physis. Grundlegung zu einer Geschichte des Wortes,* Stuttgart 1993.

78. Parmenides B 12/13 DK.

79. Democritus against Anaxagoras: A 1 DK = Diog. Laert. 9.35; self-organization: Democritus B 164 DK.

80. B. L. Van der Waerden, *Science Awakening,* New York 1961; Burkert 1972, 299–301; 428–430.

81. First documented in Hypsikles, ed. V. de Falco, M. Krause, O. Neugebauer, Göttingen 1966, pp. 36–47; it is probable that already Eudoxus, Plato's contemporary, used this scale.

82. See Chapter 4.

83. Burkert 1963; see Chapter 5 n. 60.

84. See Chapter 5 at nn. 42–51.

85. O. Neugebauer, *A History of Ancient Mathematical Astronomy* I, Berlin 1975.

86. Livingstone 1986, 78–91; cf. Burkert 1994.

87. Livingstone 1986, 10; Schibli 1990, 133.

88. The ancient tradition has produced confusion. See Schibli 17; 27–29.

89. Burkert 1963, 103.

90. Eudemus Fr. 146 Wehrli; Burkert 1972, 308–310.

91. See Kingsley 1992.

92. Plato *Epin.* 983A f.; Kingsley 1995a, 203.

93. Ezek. 1; cf. West 1971, 88 f.; Kingsley 1992.

94. Anaximander A 1 DK = Diog. Laert. 2.2 = Apollodorus FGrHist 244 F 29, see at n. 1.

95. See Introduction at n. 42.

96. Burkert 1963, 131 f.

97. See Lloyd 2000.

98. B. L. Van der Waerden, *Science Awakening*, New York 1961; qualifications in H. J. Waschkies, *Anfänge der Arithmetik im Alten Orient und bei den Griechen*, Amsterdam 1989, esp. 302–326.

99. The opposition of *gen-* and *es-* is explicit in Parmenides B 8.20 DK.

100. See Chapter 2 at n. 86.; the formula "from earth to earth" occurs in Genesis 3.19; Xenophanes B 27; Fehling 1994, 18 f.

101. *Enuma Elish* 2.65, p. 241 Dalley; cf. "to become and to be annihilated, to be and not to be" in Parmenides B 8.40.

102. *Enuma Elish* 4.22, p. 250 Dalley.

103. See C. Kahn, *The Verb Be in Ancient Greek*, Dordrecht 1973; U. Hölscher, "Der Sinn von 'sein' in der älteren griechischen Philosophie," *Sitzungsber. Heidelberg* 1976, 3. In general W. Burkert, "Revealing Nature Amidst Multiple Cultures. A Discourse with Ancient Greeks," in *The Tanner Lectures on Human Values* 21 (2000) 125–151.

104. K. Lorenz, *Die Rückseite des Spiegels. Versuch einer Naturgeschichte des menschlichen Erkennens*, Munich 1973.

4. Orpheus and Egypt

1. The standard commentaries are A. Wiedemann, *Herodots Zweites Buch mit sachlichen Erläuterungen*, Leipzig 1890, and A. B. Lloyd, *Herodotus, Book Two, I–III*, Leiden 1975–1988.

2. See Introduction at n. 45; Moeller 2000.

3. Hdt. 3.40–43.

4. See D. v. Bothmer, *The Amasis Painter and His World*, Malibu 1985;

Papers on the Amasis Painter and His World, Malibu 1987. There was one "Psammetichos son of Periandros" at Corinth, Arist. *Pol.* 1315b26, and also an ephebe "Kroisos," the so-called Kouros of Anavyssos, IG I³ 1240 = CEG I nr. 27.

5. See Bietak 2001; Kyrieleis 1996; Introduction at n. 47/48.

6. SEG 27, 1106.

7. Ibid., 1116.

8. Hdt. 2.42.2; 2.59.2; 2.144.2: cf. 2.156.5. See W. Burkert, "Herodot über die Namen der Götter: Polytheismus als historisches Problem," *Museum Helveticum* 42 (1985) 121–132; Casadio 1996. The picture of an Attic black-figure lekythos, Munich 1871 (ABV 470.103), about 500 B.C., was called "veneration of a mummy" (R. Hackl, *Archiv für Religionswissenschaft* 12 [1909] 195–203; Boardman 1964 / 1999, 151) or else "Dionysus with tragic chorus" (E. Simon, *Die Götter der Griechen,* Munich 1969, 274 fig. 263; deleted in the later editions).

9. The decisive evidence is a Linear B text from Khania, Crete; see E. Hallager, M. Vlasakis, B. P. Hallager, "New Linear B Tablets from Khania," *Kadmos* 31 (1992) 61–87.

10. Pindar Fr. 91; J. G. Griffiths, "The Flight of the Gods before Typhon: An Unrecognized Myth," *Hermes* 88 (1960) 374–376; Aesch. *Suppl.* 560: the power of Typhon in conflict with the gifts of the Nile.

11. Boardman 1980, 137 f. with fig. 162/3; LIMC Dionysos nr. 828; 829; 839–841; W. Burkert, *Homo Necans,* 1983, 200 f.; C. Auffarth, *Der drohende Untergang,* Berlin 1991, 213–220; Casadio 1996, 220, 73. The ship of Dionysus amidst sea waves: LIMC Dionysus nr. 790; the ship of Dionysus in ritual: Anthesteria at Smyrna, Aristid. Or. 17.6; Philostratus *Vit. Soph.* 17.6.

12. One usually speaks of "Lenaean vases," following A. Frickenhaus. See Burkert, *Homo Necans,* 1983, 235–238. The whole evidence is presented by F. Frontisi-Ducroux, *Le Dieu Masqué,* Paris 1991.

13. LIMC s.v. Hathor nr. 1 ff., 12 exemplars. See in particular a vase painting from Cyprus, Louvre AM 393d; V. Karageorghis and J. des Gagniers, *La Céramique chypriote de style figuré,* Rome 1974, pl. 510, "style d'Amathonte" nr. 7; A. Caubet, *La religion à Chypre dans l'antiquité,* Lyon 1979, fig. 58; LIMC Hathor nr. 16.

14. Bibliography down to 1922 in OF 345–50; until 1950: Nilsson 1952,

628f.; see Riedweg 1996. A new edition of Orphicorum Fragmenta by A. Bernabé is forthcoming (Bibliotheca Teubneriana).

15. See Zuntz 1971, 287–293.

16. Dieterich 1891, 30–41 = 1911, 91–100; 1893/1913, 84–108; Harrison 1903/1922, 572–594; Murray ibid. 659–73; see Zuntz 1971, 299–327.

17. The highest evaluation of "orfismo," close to Christian revelation, is in V. Macchioro, *Zagreus. Studi sull' Orfismo,* Bari 1920; *Zagreus. Studi intorno all' Orfismo,* Florence 1930.

18. Wilamowitz 1932, II, 192–204; I. M. Linforth, *The Arts of Orpheus,* Berkeley 1941.

19. Nilsson 1952; Dodds 1951, 147–56.

20. Zuntz 1971. He tried to neutralize the Hipponion text, Zuntz 1976, by declaring it an aberrant curiosity; this was finally refuted by the Entella text, Frel 1994.

21. Foti-Pugliese Carratelli 1973; Pugliese Carratelli 2001, I A 1. At the beginning, the reading Μνημοσύνης τόδε θρῖον (West; HPION lamella; hιρόν Pugliese Carratelli) is recommended by Aristoph. *Frogs* 134.

22. Nilsson had transferred the discussion of the gold plates to the 2nd volume of his handbook (1950, 223–27; ²1962, 235–39) and argued for a date after Plato.

23. Cassio 1994.

24. Sicily (Entella?): Frel 1994; Pugliese Carratelli 2001, I A 4 p. 76 f.; Pherai: SEG 45, 646; Pugliese Carratelli 2001, II C 2 p. 123 f.

25. Aigion: SEG 34, 338; 41, 401; Bernabé and Jiménez San Cristobal 2001, 212; 279 f.; a Dionysiac context is suggested even here by the findings, M. Osanna, *Santuari e culti dell'Acaia antica,* Naples 1996, 199f. Pella: Bernabé and Jiménez San Cristobal 2001, 211 f.; 279 f., see n. 40. Sfakaki: I. Gavrilaki, Y. Z. Tzifopoulos, "An Orphic-Dionysiac Gold Epistomion from Sfakaki near Rethymno," *Bulletin de Correspondance Hellénique* 122 (1998) 343–355.

26. *Archaeological Reports* 1988/89, 93.

27. Rusajeva 1978, see at n. 60.

28. *Zeitschrift für Papyrologie und Epigraphik* 47, 1982 appendix; Laks–Most 1997, with complete bibliography and English translation. As against the text of 1982 the number of columns has been increased by 4; in this

chapter the new count is adopted. A new English translation, on the basis of a revised text, is given by R. Janko, *Classical Philology* 96 (2001) 18–32; the new text, based on all the available evidence, with translation, has now been published by R. Janko, "The Derveni Papyrus: An Interim Text," *ZPE* 141 (2002) 1–62.

29. Archaeological publication: P. G. Themelis, G. P. Touratsoglou, *Oi taphoi tou Derbeniou,* Athens 1997.

30. See at nn. 82—83.

31. The comprehensive edition is due to Pugliese Carratelli 1993; 2001; a selection is presented in Scarpi 2001; collection, Spanish translation and commentary in Bernabé and Jiménez San Cristobal 2001. Among the extensive bibliography, see esp. Borgeaud 1991; Bottini 1992; Graf 1993; Giangiulio 1994; Dettori 1996; Riedweg 1998.

32. Pugliese Carratelli 2001, I A 1, 15 f., p. 40.

33. Ibid., II B 3/4, pp. 114–117.

34. Ibid., II C 2, p. 123.

35. Plato *Republic* 364b–366ab: 366a; Pindar Fr. 131a.

36. See Burkert 1987b, 33.

37. Plato *Republic* 364b–365a.

38. P. Derv. col. XX.

39. Graf 1974, 40–50.

40. *Supplementum Hellenisticum* 705, 22; Burkert 1974, 85. Cf. Hegesippos AP 7.545: the way to the right leads to Rhadamanthys; gold plate from Pella, above n. 25: "Poseidippos the initiate to Persephone." This might rather belong to the poet's grandfather; see Dickie 1995; Rossi 1996.

41. Funerary relief, Nilsson 1961 pl. 4.1, IG XII 1, 141 = Peek 1916. It may belong to the Peripatetic philosopher Hieronymus of Rhodes.

42. *Mystica vada* Accius fr. 687 Ribbeck = Varro *Ling. Lat.* 7.19.

43. Pindar Fr. 131a, cf. above n. 35.

44. Pindar Fr. 137. As it is addressed to an Athenian, it will point to Eleusis.

45. Pugliese Carratelli 2001, II B 3/4, p. 114–117.

46. Hints in Plato *Crat.* 400c = OF 8 and in *Phd.* 62b = OF 7; Pythagorean "akousma" in Iambl. VP 85; Arist. Fr. 60; the "mourning of Persephone," Pindar Fr. 133, cf. Burkert 1977, 443. "Recompense" ($\pi o\iota\nu\acute{\eta}$) paid or

released is mentioned in two gold plates, II A 2 (Thurioi) and II C 2 (Pherai).

47. Transmigration as known from Pindar, Herodotus, Empedocles, and Plato (note Plato *Leg.* 870d: retribution as "justice of Rhadamanthys" according to the teachings of *teletai*) is not explicitly described in the gold plates. But the forbidden spring where "souls, coming down, cool themselves" (texts I A 1 from Hipponion and I A 4 from Entella), in contrast to the "Lake of Memory," must be a place of "Forgetting" (cf. *Lethe* Plato *Republic* 621a), and the "flight from the wheel" in the text II B 1 (Thurioi, Pugliese Carratelli 2001, p. 102 f.; Zuntz 1971, 318–22) can hardly be understood otherwise than with reference to transmigration. "Relief" from the "wheel" appears in Orphic verses too, which Plato seems to have known, OF 229, 230; Plato *Leg.* 713e.

48. Jeffery 1961/1990, 240 nr. 12; Burkert 1977, 438; 1994, 27.

49. II A 1 and II A 2, Pugliese Carratelli 2001, p. 98 f.; 100 f.

50. I A 2, Pugliese Carratelli 2001, p. 67 f.

51. Pindar *Ol.* 2.70, following evidently the variant text of Hesiod, *Erga* 173 a–e.

52. II B 2, Pugliese Carratelli 2001, p. 112 f.

53. II B 1 and II B 2, Pugliese Carratelli 2001, p. 103; 113.

54. Hdt. 2.81; see at n. 118.

55. Tsantsanoglou 1997, 114 n. 38; SEG 45, 646; II C 2, Pugliese Carratelli 2001, p. 123 f.; see n. 24.

56. Hermann Diels called the gold plates "passports for the dead," "ein orphischer Totenpaß," in *Philotesia für P. Kleinert,* Berlin 1907, 41–49.

57. The same duplication is found in a graffito from Olbia, about 300 B.C., Dubois 1996 nr. 96; it refers to a cult group of "fellows of the North" *(boreikoi thiasitai)* and reads: Life–Life, Apollo–Apollo, Helios–Helios, World–World, Light–Light.

58. In the Cabirian mysteries at Thebes a *pais* together with *Kabiros* is at the center; see an often published vase painting, Nilsson 1967 pl. 48.1; LIMC VIII s.v. Megaloi Theoi nr. 25.

59. OF 31; 1 B 23 DK; J. Hordern, "Notes on the Orphic Papyrus from Gurôb (P. Gurôb 1. Pack² 2464)," *Zeitschrift für Papyrologie und Epigraphik* 129 (2000) 131–140.

60. Rusajeva 1978, 87–104; West 1983, 17–20; Dettori 1996; new edition by Dubois 1996, nr. 94; new reading by Vinogradov 1991. The last letter of ΟΡΦΙΚΟΙ is unclear.

61. Pindar Fr. 137, see at n. 44.

62. Heraclitus B 15 DK; see Chapter 5 n. 29.

63. Heraclitus B 14; 28 DK.

64. Hdt. 4.78–80; Burkert 1977, 434; 1987b, 33.

65. F. Sokolowski, *Lois sacrées de l'Asie Mineure,* Paris 1955, nr. 48; Burkert 1987b, 33.

66. Rusajeva 1978; Dubois 1996, nr. 92: ΔΗΜΩΝΑΣΣΑ ΛΗΝΑΙΟ ΕΤΑΙ ΚΑΙ ΛΗΝΑΙΟΣ ΔΗΜΟΚΛΟ ΕΤΑΙ; cf. Burkert 1987b, 22; the second Lenaios is probably son of Demonassa and grandson of the first Lenaios. Note that SEG 42, 721 has a wrong date, "late fifth cent. B.C.?," referring to F. Tinnefeld, *Zeitschrift für Papyrologie und Epigraphik* 38 (1980), 70 f., who says "Ende 6. Jh." ΕΤΑΙ also as graffito on a scyphos from Berezan at Olbia, 6th cent., SEG 32, 779; Dettori 1996, 302.

67. Standard publications are A. D. Trendall, *The Red-Figured Vases of Lucania, Campania, and Sicily,* Oxford 1967; A. D. Trendall, A. Cambitoglou, *The Red-Figured Vases of Apulia I–III,* Oxford 1978/82; on "orphism" in these vases see Schmidt 1975; Schmidt-Trendall-Cambitoglou 1976.

68. S. I. Johnston, T. J. McNiven, "Dionysos and the Underworld in Toledo Museum" *Helveticum* 53 (1996) 25–36.

69. This myth is localized at Lerna, Paus. 2.37.5.

70. Hor. *Carm.* 2.19.29–31. It is true that Horace's Bacchus has horns, a type of imagery which is not found in Apulian vase painting.

71. Schmidt 1975, plates 10–13; Bianchi 1976, fig. 69–71.

72. Schmidt 1975, plates 1–6.

73. British Museum F 270; Trendall-Cambitoglou (n. 67) 18/318; Schmidt 1975, 120 f. with pl. 14.

74. Published by Schmidt 1975, pl. 7–8; Schmidt-Trendall-Cambitoglou 1976, 32 f., pl. 11.

75. A terracotta group of Orpheus and the Sirens, almost life size, came to the Paul Getty Museum, apparently from an Apulian chamber tomb: *The P. J. Getty Museum. Handbook of the Collection,* Malibu 1986, 33; A. Bottini,

P. G. Guzzo, "Orfeo e le sirene al Getty Museum," *Ostraka* 2 (1993) 52; cf.
W. Burkert, "Orphism and Bacchic Mysteries: New Evidence and Old
Problems of Interpretation," *The Center for Hermeneutical Studies,* Colloquy
28, Berkeley 1977, 31.

76. Already remarked by Rohde 1898, II 390 f. (who had only indirect
knowledge of the Book of the Dead and knew few of the gold plates);
Zuntz 1971, 370–376; see E. A. W. Budge, *The Egyptian Book of the Dead,*
London 1895, 314 f.; E. Hornung, *Das Totenbuch der Ägypter,* Zurich 1979,
128–130, section 58/59.

77. I B 1–6, cf. I B 7 in Pugliese Carratelli 2001. "May Osiris give you
fresh water" is a formula attested later, mostly in Greek, from Egypt to
Rome, Burkert 1987b, 26 n. 75.

78. G. Maass-Lindemann, M. Maass, "Ägyptisierende Amulett-
Blechbänder aus Andalusien," *Madrider Mitteilungen* 35 (1994) 140–156;
G. Hölbl, *Ägyptisches Kulturgut im phönikischen und punischen Sardinien,*
Leiden 1986, 338–53; "Ägyptisches Kulturgut auf Malta und Gozo," *Sitz-
ungsberichte Wien* 538, 1989, 104–123; Kotansky 1991, 115. One early gold
plate, 8th–7th century, in Guzzo Amadasi 1967, 121, Sardegna nr. 38, from a
tophet, bears a short inscription (7 letters).

79. Hdt. 2.49; cf. at n. 121.

80. Origin from heaven, "my name is Asterios," I A 3, 12, Pugliese
Carratelli 2001, p. 73 f. (Pharsalus); see Chapter 5 at n. 47; Heraclitus B 14
combines *bakchoi* and *magoi;* see also at n. 62 on the Oblia graffiti and
Heraclitus.

81. C. Watkins, *How to Kill a Dragon,* Oxford 1995, 284–291, with reference to Hoffner-Beckmann 1990, 32 f.

82. Burkert 1968.

83. Stesimbrotos Περὶ Τελετῶν (FGrHist 107 F 12–20) was proposed
by Burkert 1986 on the basis of very small textual coincidence.

84. See Obbink 1994, following A. Henrichs, *Cronace Ercolanesi* 5 (1975)
18: Philodemus writes κἀν τοῖς Ὕμνοις δὲ Ὀρφεὺς παρὰ Φιλοχόρωι
Γῆν καὶ Δήμητρα τὴν αὐτὴν Ἑστίαι, which evidently corresponds to
the quotation "in the hymns" P.Derv. col. 22. This could be understood as
if Philochorus himself were the author of Derveni, but that is excluded by
the chronological criteria of style and contents.

85. West 1983, 114 f., followed by Scarpi 2002, 366–369 (Orfismo A 7).

86. OF 334: θύρας ἐπίθεσθε, βέβηλοι; Plato *Symp.* 218b = OF 13; P.Derv. col. 7[3].9, Laks–Most 1997, 95. The first part of the verse has two variants, Ἀείσω συνετοῖσι OF 334 and φθέγξομαι οἷς θέμις ἐστίν OF 245, cf. Tsantsanoglou 1997, 125f.; the text with συνετοί seems to be presupposed by Pindar *Ol.* 2.85 and Bacchylides 3.85.

87. Col. 14[10]. 6: Οὐρανὸς Εὐφρονίδης, ὃς πρώτιστος βασίλευσεν; cf. Eudemus Fr. 150 Wehrli; Arist. *Met.* 1071b27.

88. OF 220 = Olympiod. *In Phd.* 1.3, p. 41f. Westerink; see n. 112. The "Orphic" theogony usually constructed from Aristophanes *Birds* 690 ff. = OF 1 is not compatible with the Derveni theogony, which has no place for a "world egg."

89. Col. 15[11].6: ἐκ τοῦ δὴ Κρόνος αὖτις, ἔπειτα δὲ μητίετα Ζεύς.

90. Col. 13[9].4: <βασιλῆος> αἰδοῖον κατέπινεν, ὃς αἰθέρα ἔχθορε πρῶτος.

91. καὶ δαίμονα κυδρὸν|αἰδοῖον κατέπινεν West 1983, 85 f. cf. 114; he is followed by Laks and Most 1997, 15 f.; but see Janko 2001 (n. 28) and A. Bernabé, *De Tales a Demócrito*, Madrid 2001; for αἰδοῖον "phallus" see Heraclitus B 15 DK.

92. ἀρχὴν ἐν χείρεσσ' ἔλαβεν καὶ δαίμονα κυδρόν col. 8[4].5; 7; 10; col. 9[5].10. On this *daimon* see Chapter 5 n. 82.

93. Col. 14[19].1 … ἐχθόρηι τὸν λαμπρότατόν τε καὶ λευκότατον.

94. Aesch. fr. 15 Radt = Hesych s.v. θρώσκων· κνώδαλα, paraphrase: ἐκθορίζων καὶ σπερματίζων. P.Derv. col. 21[17].1 has θορνηι, with reference to "begettings" of Zeus, a *hapax,* hence controversial, possibly meaning "jumping" as a sexual act.

95. Cf. Diod. 1.22.6 on the "hidden phallus" of Osiris, said to play its role in *teletai* and sacrifices of the Egyptians.

96. See Introduction at n. 10; Chapter 3 n. 66.

97. Hes. *Theog.* 886–900. The Metis episode probably occurs in the Derveni text too, col. 15[11].13 (very fragmentary).

98. OF 199, main texts Procl. *Tim.* I.407 f.; Orph. Hymn. 49; see M.-C. Trémouille, *ᵈHebat. Une divinité Syro-anatolienne,* Florence 1997.

99. See Bickel 1994, 72–83.

100. Hdt. 2.137; 139; 152.

101. Lichtheim I, 52–56; *Sources Orientales: Naissance* 62–64; cf. Pyramid texts 1248a ff.; cosmogony of On, West 1983, 188 f.

102. ... πρωτογόνου βασιλέως αἰδοίου· τοῦ δ᾽ ἄρα πάντες
ἀθάνατοι προσέφυν μάκαρες θεοὶ ἠδὲ θέαιναι
καὶ ποταμοὶ καὶ κρῆναι ἐπήρατοι, ἄλλα τε πάντα
ὅσσα τοτ᾽ ἦν γεγαῶτ(α)· αὐτὸς δ᾽ ἄρα μοῦνος ἔγεντο.

103. See A. Erman, *Die Religion der Ägypter,* Berlin 1934, 310; 325; Hornung 2000.

104. Hymn to Ninurta, which makes a whole pantheon into limbs of Ninurta's body, Von Soden SAHG 258 f.; Forster 619 f.; B. N. Porter, ed., *One God or Many?,* Casco Bay 2000, 240–251.

105. OF 167:
καὶ ποταμοὶ καὶ πόντος ἀπείριτος, ἄλλα τε πάντα,
πάντες τ᾽ ἀθάνατοι μάκαρες θεοὶ ἠδὲ θέαιναι,
ὅσσα τ᾽ ἔην᾽ γεγαῶτα καὶ ὕστερον ὁππόσ᾽ ἔμελλεν ...

106. OF 168, combined with Iranian and Indian evidence by Reitzenstein-Schaeder 1926, 69–103; A. Olerud, *L'idée de macrocosmos et de microcosmos dans le "Timée" de Platon,* Uppsala 1951, 114–128; 129–152.

107. Col. 17[13]; 19[15], corresponding to OF 21a.1; 2; 7 and 168.1; 2; 5. Plato *Leg.* 715e quotes the verse of col. 17[13] 12 = OF 21a.2 = 168.2.

108. Ζεὺς πρῶτος γένετο, Ζεὺς ὕστατος ἀργικέραυνος.
Ζεὺς ἀρχή, Ζεὺς μέσσα, Διὸς δ᾽ ἐκ παντα τέτυκται.
Ζεὺς βασιλεύς, Ζεὺς ἀρχὸς ἁπάντων ...

109. Most important is Plato *Phlb.* 66c = OF 14.

110. Col. 23[19].4; see also OF 81.

111. See Bickel 1994, 106 f.; 145.

112. OF 220 = Olympiod. *In Phd.* 1.3 p. 41 f. Westerink.

113. See Brisson 1992: a very late, alchemistic text?

114. *Atrahasis* I.213–217; 228–230; *Enuma Elish* VI.1–34; Burkert 1992, 126 f.

115. Burkert 1967.

116. Col. 23; POxy. 221.9 = Schol. Ilias ed. Erbse V 93.

117. See A. Bernabé, "Referencias a textos órficos en Diodoro," in L. Torraca, ed., *Scritti in onore di Italo Gallo,* Naples 2002, 67–96. Interesting passages are Diod. 1.21–23; 1.96–97; the hidden phallus 1.22.7; Kronos and the Titans 1.97.5.

118. Hdt. 2.81.2. The "long" version is defended by Burkert 1972, 127 f.; against this L. Zhmud', "Orphism and Graffiti from Olbia," *Hermes* 120 (1992) 159–168: 164 refers to the graffito *Orphikoi* from Olbia (see n. 60) and postulates the same form for Herodotus, hence "Orphics and Pythagoreans" should be masculines, and the short version should be original. I still think the argument of Dodds 1951, 169 n. 80 holds true: τούτων τῶν ὀργίων in Herodotus' continuation points to neutra, in four terms: Orphic-Bacchic-Egyptian-Pythagorean.

119. On *orgia* see A. Motte, V. Pirenne-Delforge *Kernos* 5 (1992) 119–140; *orgia* in the context of mysteries appear already in the old Homeric hymn to Demeter (273, 476).

120. Gold plates of Hipponion type, see at n. 21; cf. Philolaos A 30 DK, Iambl. VP 165, Diod. 10.5.1 = 58 D 1 DK, Diog. Laert 8.4 = 14, 8 DK; see Zuntz 1971, 380 f. A strange ritual rule "not to roast the cooked" is attested for some *Telete,* probably Bacchic, Arist. *Probl. Ined.* 3.43 Bussemaker, and for the Pythgoreans, Iambl. VP 154, cf. Ath. 656b; see M. Detienne, *Dionysos mis à mort,* Paris 1977, 161–207.

121. Hdt. 2.49.1; see at n. 8; 79. Herodotus also holds that transmigration is Egyptian (2.123).

5. The Advent of the Magi

1. For recent comprehensive accounts of Achaemenid history see Högemann 1992; Briand 1996; Wiesehöfer 1996. Miller 1997 gives a detailed survey from the Athenian side.

2. See Boardman 2000.

3. See also Burkert 1995,

4. See Sources in Translation. The place name is also transcribed as *Bisutun.*

5. A. H. Anquetil-Duperron, *Zend-Avesta. Ouvrage de Zoroastre,* Paris 1771; cf. R. Schwab, *Vie d'Anquetil-Duperron,* Paris 1934.

6. M. Boye, *A History of Zoroastrianism* I, Leiden 1975; Gnoli 2000, *contra* Gnoli 1994, 472 f; cf. Kingsley 1990; Stausberg 2002.

7. FGrHist 765 F 32, discussed by Kingsley 1995a. "Mitra," with strange misunderstanding, is mentioned by Hdt. 1.131.

8. See at nn. 64–69; on the book *Magikos* (Antisthenes?) see n. 23.

Aristoxenus fr. 13 writes *Zaratas,* Diod. 1.94.2 *Zathraustes.* Further references in Deinon FGrHist 650 F 5; Eudoxus Fr. 342 Lasserre; Justin. 1.1.9, perhaps from Ctesias. See Kingsley 1995a; De Jong 1997—at the time unaware of the Derveni papyrus; he disregards the decree of Dareios about reading his text in the provinces.

9. See Reitzenstein-Schaeder 1926; Widengren 1965 and 1983.

10. Xen. Anab. 5, 3, 6. See W. Burkert, "Die Artemis der Epheser," in H. Friesinger, F. Krinzinger, ed., *100 Jahre Österreichische Forschungen in Ephesos,* Vienna 1999, 59–70: 62 f. On the etymology of Megabyxos see n. 15. The name Megabyxos does not appear in Nilsson's *History of Greek Religion.*

11. Strabo 14 p. 641.

12. *Pompa* of Megabyzus by Apelles, Pliny *Nat. Hist.* 35.93, cf. Plut. *Adul.* 58d; *Tranqu.* 471f; Ael. *Varia Hist.* 2.2 (Zeuxis); funeral of Megabyxus, painting by Antidotus in Ephesus, Pliny *Nat. Hist.* 35.132.

13. Behistun inscription § 68, preserved in Persian and in Akkadian; Megabyxos in Hdt. 3.70.3.

14. See RE s.v.; Deinon FGrHist 690 F 1 transcribes his name as Βαγάβαζος.

15. F. Justi, *Iranisches Namenbuch,* Marburg 1895, 56 f.; Liddell-Scott s.v. μεγάβυξος; E. Benveniste, *Titres et noms propres en Iranien ancien,* Paris 1966, 108–115; Miller, *Language* 44 (1968) 846; M. Mayrhofer, *Iranisches Personennamenbuch* I.2, Vienna 1979, 16.

16. Cf. Ephorus FGrHist 70 F 58 on a man from Ephesus who deserted Croesus for Cyrus.

17. Polyb. 21.37.4–7, 190 B.C. The Branchidai, priests of Apollo's sanctuary at Didyma, made their deal with the Persians, too, and hence were accused of "medismos"; see H. W. Parke, "The Massacre of the Branchidae," *Journal of Hellenic Studies* 105 (1985) 59–68.

18. R. Meiggs, D. Lewis, *A Selection of Greek Historical Inscriptions to the End of the Fifth Century B.C.,* Oxford 1969, nr. 12, pp. 20 f.

19. Strabo 14 p. 634.

20. Plut. *Alex.* 3.7, cf. Cic. *Nat. deo.* 2.69, *Div.* 1.47.

21. See Chapter 3 n. 2.

22. See Graf 1994, 31–45; Graf 1995.

23. Arist. Fr. 32–36, esp. Arist. Fr. 36 = Diog. Laert. 1.6–8; on the question of authorship: Suda s.v. Antisthenes = Arist. Fr. 33; see also Porph. *Abst.* 4.16: μάγοι = οἱ περὶ τὸ θεῖον σοφοί. Since for moderns a book with a title *Magikos* is not thought to be "genuine," it is usually disregarded.

24. Plut. *Them.* 29.16; note that this information is independent from Herodotus and could be older than his work; Themistocles died about 459/ 8.

25. Hippocr. *Morb. Sacr.* VI.354 Littré.

26. Soph. *O. T.* 387, parallel to ἀγύρτης.

27. Eur. *Or.* 1496; cf. Plato *Polit.* 280d.

28. Gorgias B 11, 10 DK.

29. Heraclitus B 14 DK = FR. 87 Marcovich, p. 465–467: νυκτιπόλοις μάγοις; Marcovich, following Karl Reinhardt, pleads for athetesis; contra, Tsantsanoglou 1997, 115, 43. The qualification "swarming at night" is unique and cannot be explained; this might be its a mark of authenticity. Heraclitus' special dependence on Iranian sources has often been assumed, concerning above all the role of "fire" and of divine order, Greek *logos* and *nomos,* Avestan *asha.* See West 1971, 111–202. Zoroastrian fire worship is not attested before Hellenistic Asia Minor and becomes central only in the Sassanid epoch.

30. Inscription of Behistun (cf. n. 4) § 11, vgl. §§ 13; 14; 16; 52; 68.

31. Yasna 65.7.

32. Koch 1992, 279 f.

33. Bidez and Cumont 1938.

34. KAI 265, Greek and Aramaic, about 1st cent. A.D.

35. Pliny *Nat. Hist.* 30.16 f., cf. Tac. *Ann.* 15.29. That the *magoi* at Bethlehem, Matthew 2, are a reflection of Tiridates' arrival is an old idea.

36. See Brown III 2001, 91 f.

37. R. C. Zaehner, *Zurvan. A Zoroastrian Dilemma,* Oxford 1955; Widengren 1965, 283–295; West 1971, 30–33.

38. Reitzenstein-Schaeder 1926, 38–68; considered a very clear case of oriental import by Heubeck 1955. This may well be the case, but the Iranian Pahlevi sources are probably of secondary value. See Burkert 1983b; Widengren 1983, 151–154.

39. A. Goetze, "Persische Weisheit in griechischem Gewande," *Zeit-*

schrift für Indologie und Iranistik 2 (1923) 60–98, 167–177; new discussions by J. Duchesne-Guillemin, *Harvard Theological Review* 49 (1956) 115–122 and 1966, 427, with totally conflicting judgments; see also Momigliano 1975, 128 f.

40. On what follows see Bremmer 2002.

41. Gilgamesh XII 94 f., p. 123 Dalley, p. 732 f. George.

42. Ed. Piras 2000.

43. H. Dörrie, *Der Königskult des Antiochos von Kommagene im Lichte neuer Inschriftenfunde,* Göttingen 1964, 65; vgl. 35: "He led the imperishable nature of the soul up to the eternal house of the blessed gods."

44. Yasna 31.7; 21.

45. Yasna 43.3; 35.11.

46. Yasna 51.15.

47. L. Rougier, *L'origine astronomique de la croyance pythagoricienne en l'immortalité céleste des âmes,* Cairo 1933, cf. Burkert 1972, 358–360.

48. Epicharmus 23 B 9; 22 DK = 213; 254 Kassel-Austin.

49. Eur. *Erechtheus* fr. 65,72 in C. Austin, *Nova Fragmenta Euripidea,* Berlin 1968, 38.

50. So Eur. *Suppl.* 532: πνεῦμα μὲν πρὸς αἰθέρα.

51. IG I² 945 = I³ 1179 = CEG I nr. 10.

52. Eur. Fr. 839 = Anaxagoras A 112 DK. The idea of return appears in the Bible, Qohelet 12.7 "The spirit *(ruah)* goes back to god"; some think this must be (Hellenistic) interpolation.

53. Diogenes of Apollonia A 19.42 DK = Theophr. *Sens.* 42, cf. Diogenes B 3 DK.

54. Xen. *Mem.* 1.4.8.

55. Heracles with *Hebe,* personified "Youth," as his consort, LIMC s.v. Herakles nr. 3331; A. F. Laurens in C. Jourdain-Annequin, C. Bonnet, ed., *Héraclès, les femmes et le féminin,* Brussels 1996, 240.

56. *Od.* 11.602 f., denounced as interpolation by Schol.

57. Paus. 3.19.4.

58. Nilsson 1967, pl. 10.3.

59. See Chapter 4.

60. Burkert 1963, cf. Chapter 3 at n. 89; West 1971, 85–93. West observed that the passage of *Denkart* 7.2.3 quoted 1963, 108, refers to "the Rev-

elation," i.e. a lost part of the Avesta, which means that this is a source not from the 9th cent. A.D. but from the Achaemenid period.

61. See Chapter 3 at n. 86; Burkert 1995, cf. Burkert 1963, 103; 1972, 309 n. 57.

62. Ezekiel 1; West 1971, 88 f.; cf. Kingsley 1992; Chapter 3 n. 93. An older form of heavenly structure and ascent, without the stars, is reconstructed by M. West, "Darius Ascent to Paradise," *Indo-Iranian Journal* 45 (2002) 51–57.

63. Burkert 1963, 131 f.; Chapter 3 at n. 89/90.

64. Plut. *Is.* 46–47, 369 D-370 C = Theopompus FGrHist 115 F 65; Bidez and Cumont 1938, II 70–79. See also J. Hani, "Plutarque en face du dualisme iranien," *Revue des Études grecques* 77 (1964) 489–525; U. Bianchi, *Selected Essays on Gnosticism, Dualism and Mysteriosophy,* Leiden 1978.

65. Hippol. *Ref.* 1.2.12 = Aristoxenus Fr. 13 Wehrli. See Kingsley 1990.

66. Damascius *Princ.* 125, I p. 322 Ruelle = Eudemus Fr. 150 Wehrli.

67. Arist. *Met.* 1091b10.

68. Plato *Leg.* 896 DE, 906 A; Plut. *Procr.* 1014 D; *Is.* 370 EF.

69. J. Kerschensteiner, *Platon und der Orient,* Stuttgart 1945; see also J. Bidez, *Eos ou Platon et l'orient,* Brussels 1945; W. J. W. Koster, *Le mythe de Platon, de Zarathoustra et des Chaldéens,* Leiden 1951; W. Spoerri, "Encore Platon et l'orient," *Revue de Philologie* 31 (1957) 209–233.

70. Empedocles B 30 DK.

71. Xanthos FGrHist 765 F 33; Kingsley 1995a, 185–191.

72. Gorgias A 3 DK = Empedocles A 1 § 59 DK = Diog. Laert. 8.59; Empedocles B 111 DK. See above n. 25.

73. Hdt. 3.125–137; nr. 19 DK.

74. Tsantsanoglou 1997; see Chapter 4 n. 28.

75. 3.7: εἰσὶν ὅπωσπερ ἄνδρες ἄδικοι. Tsantsanoglou 1997, 96 translates as "sinners" who "do not escape punishment"; but what about ὅπωσπερ?

76. Col. 5.10: ἀπιστίη δὲ κἀμαθίη ταὐτόν.

77. Col. 18[14].5.

78. 1   [εὐ]χαὶ καὶ θυc[ί]αι μ[ειλ]ίccουσι τὰ[c ψυχάc,]

    2   ἐπ[ωιδὴ δ]ὲ μάγων δύν[α]ται δαίμονας ἐμ[ποδὼν

    3   γι[νομένου]c μεθιστάναι· δαίμονες ἐμπο[δὼν εἰcι

4 ψ[υχαῖc ἐχθ]ροί. τὴν θυc[ία]ν τούτου ἔνεκε[ν] π[οιοὺc]ι[ν
5 οἱ μάγοι ὡcπερεὶ ποινὴν ἀποδιδόντεc· τοῖc δὲ
6 ἱεροῖ[c] ἐπιcπένδουσιν ὕ[δω]ρ καὶ γάλα, ἐξ ὧνπερ καὶ τὰc
7 χοὰc ποιοῦσι. ἀνάριθμα [κα]ὶ πολυόμφαλα τὰ πόπανα
8 θύουcιν, ὅτι καὶ αἱ ψυχα[ὶ ἀν]άριθμοί εἰcι. μύcται
9 Εὐμενίcι προθύουcι κ[ατὰ τὰ] αὐτὰ μάγοιc· Εὐμενίδεc
   γὰρ
10 ψυχαί εἰcιν· ὧν ἔνεκ[εν τὸν μέλλοντ]α θεοῖc θύειν
11 ὀ[ρ]νίθ[ε]ιον πρότερον [c.11] ιcποτε[ ]ται . . .

79. Suggestions in line 4 are ψυχῶν φρουροί (ἔφοροι), ψυχαὶ τιμωροί, ψυχαὶ ἀνίεροι (Tsantsanoglou 1997, 113).

80. On Erinys as "soul" Rohde 1898, I 267–270; Harrison 1903/1922, 214 f.

81. Tsantsanoglou 1997, 114. On the Gurob papyrus see Chapter 4 n. 59; 1 B 23, 18 DK: ἔτεμον ποινάς.

82. Tsantsanoglou 1997, 113 surveys the Iranian evidence and refers to the *fravashi*. In one verse of Orpheus quoted (col. 8[4].5; 7; 10; 9[5].10; Chapter 4 at n. 92) a "powerful daimon," δαίμων κυδρός, is transmitted from Kronos to Zeus. This might be the Splendour of kingship, *xvarena*, of Iranian tradition (on which see Wiesehöfer 1996, 167).

83. Diog. Laert. 8.32 = Alexander Polyhistor FGrHist 273 F 93 = 58 B 1a DK; see Burkert 1972, 53.

84. Thales A 22; 23 DK; cf. Heraclitus A 1.7 DK.

85. Arist. *An.* 404a18 = 58 B 40 DK; 403b20 = 67 A 28 DK.

86. Diogenes of Apollonia A 19.42 DK, see n. 53.

87. Burkert 1968, confirmed by the fragments published later.

88. Diog. Laert. 1.6. On the question of Diogenes' sources see Wehrli on Sotion Fr. 35/36.

89. Diog. Laert. 1.7.

90. W. Burkert, "Air-Imprints or Eidola. Democritus' Aetiology of Vision," *Illinois Class. Studies 2* (1977) 97–109.

91. Democrit A 77 DK = Plut. *Q.Conv.* 735A; B 166 DK = Sextus *Adv. Math.* 9.19; Plut. *Aem.Paul* 1 (not in DK). Ancients alleged Democritus had been a pupil of the *mágoi*, Diog. Laert. 9.34; Hippol. *Ref.* 1.13; Pliny *Nat. Hist.* 24.160; Ael. *Varia Hist.* 4.20; Clement *Strom.* 1.69; Philostr. *V. Soph.*

10; we do not know whether this was based on reliable information or was just a conclusion drawn from the "magical" writings of Pseudo-Democritus (68 B 300 DK).

92. Hdt. 1.131.

93. Diogenes von Apollonia A 8 DK = Philod. *De pietate* p. 70 Gomperz; Eur. *Tro* 886.

94. See Archelaus A 12 DK.

95. Democritus B 30 DK; the original text is found in Clement *Protr.* 68: πάντα Δία μυθέεσθαι (indirect speech); using his excerpt again, *Strom.* 5.103, Clement wrote πάντα Ζεὺς μυθεῖται which is nonsense. The Derveni text now confirms the correct wording.

96. Col. 19[15]: ἐπεὶ . . . ἐν [ἔκ]αστογ κέκ[λητ]αι ἀπὸ τοῦ ἐπικρατοῦντος, Ζεὺ[ς] πάντα κατὰ τὸν αὐτὸν λόγον ἐκλήθη.

Index